HAIL HOLY QUEEN

Hail Holy Queen!

HAIL HOLY QUEEN

An Explanation of the Salve Regina
And the Role of the Blessed Mother
In Our Salvation

THE MANY AND ABUNDANT GRACES DISPENSED BY
THE MOTHER OF GOD TO HER DEVOTED CLIENTS,
FROM "THE GLORIES OF MARY"

By

St. Alphonsus Liguori

*Bishop, Confessor, Doctor of the Church and
Founder of the Congregation of the Most Holy Redeemer*

TAN BOOKS AND PUBLISHERS, INC.
Rockford, Illinois 61105

Nihil Obstat: Thomas L. Kinkead
                Censor Librorum

Imprimatur: ✠Michael Augustine
                Archbishop of New York
                New York
                October 10, 1896

Library of Congress Catalog Card No.: 95-60489

ISBN: 0-89555-523-9

Printed and bound in the United States of America.

TAN BOOKS AND PUBLISHERS, INC.
P. O. Box 424
Rockford, Illinois 61105
1995

Salve Regina

SALVE REGINA, Mater Misericordiae! Vita, dulcedo, et spes nostra, salve! Ad te clamamus, exsules filii Hevae. Ad te suspiramus, gementes et flentes in hac lacrymarum valle. Eia ergo, advocata nostra, illos tuos misericordes oculos ad nos converte! Et Jesum, benedictum fructum ventris tui, nobis post hoc exsilium ostende, O clemens, O pia, O dulcis Virgo Maria.

Hail Holy Queen

HAIL HOLY QUEEN, Mother of mercy, our life, our sweetness and our hope! To thee do we cry, poor banished children of Eve. To thee do we send up our sighs, mourning and weeping in this valley of tears. Turn then, most gracious advocate, thine eyes of mercy towards us. And after this our exile, show unto us the blessed Fruit of thy womb, Jesus, O clement, O loving, O sweet Virgin Mary.

CONTENTS.

CHAPTER I.

Salve Regina, Mater Misericordiæ!

MARY, OUR QUEEN, OUR MOTHER.

CHAPTER II.

Vita, Dulcedo.

MARY, OUR LIFE, OUR SWEETNESS.

CHAPTER III.

Spes nostra! salve.

MARY, OUR HOPE.

CHAPTER IV.

Ad te clamamus, exsules filii Evæ.

MARY, OUR HELP.

CHAPTER V.

Ad te suspiramus, gementes et flentes in hac lacrymarum valle.

MARY, OUR MEDIATRESS.

CHAPTER VI.

Eia ergo, Advocata nostra!

MARY, OUR ADVOCATE.

CHAPTER VII.

Illos tuos misericordes oculos ad nos converte.

MARY, OUR GUARDIAN.

CHAPTER VIII.

Et Jesum, benedictum Fructum ventris tui nobis post hoc exilium ostende.

MARY, OUR SALVATION.

CHAPTER IX.

O Clemens, O Pia !

CLEMENCY AND COMPASSION OF MARY.

CHAPTER X.

O dulcis Virgo Maria.

SWEETNESS OF THE NAME OF MARY.

EXPLANATION OF THE SALVE REGINA.

CHAPTER I.

Salve, Regina, Mater Misericordiæ!

HAIL, HOLY QUEEN, MOTHER OF MERCY!

MARY, OUR QUEEN, OUR MOTHER.

I. How great should be our Confidence in Mary, who is the Queen of Mercy.

As the glorious Virgin Mary has been raised to the dignity of Mother of the King of kings, it is not without reason that the Church honors her, and wishes her to be honored by all, with the glorious title of Queen.

"If the Son is a king," says St. Athanasius, "the Mother who begot Him is rightly and truly considered a Queen and Sovereign." *   "No sooner had Mary," says St. Bernardine of Siena, "consented to be Mother of the Eternal Word, than she merited by this consent to be made Queen of the world and of all creatures." †   "Since the flesh of Mary" remarks the Abbot Arnold of Chartres, "was not different from that of Jesus, how can the royal dignity of the Son

---

* *Serm. de Deip.*   † *Pro Fest. V. M.* s. 5, c. 3.

be denied to the Mother?" * " Hence we must consider the glory of the Son, not only as being common to His Mother, but as one with her." †

And if Jesus is the King of the universe, Mary is
also its Queen. "And as Queen," says the Abbot
Rupert, "she possesses, by right, the whole kingdom
of her Son." ‡   Hence St. Bernardine of Siena concludes that "as many creatures as there are who serve
God, so many they are who serve Mary : for as angels
and men, and all things that are in heaven and on
earth, are subject to the empire of God, so are they
also under the dominion of Mary!" §   The Abbot
Guerricus, addressing himself to the divine Mother
on this subject, says : "Continue, Mary, continue
to dispose with confidence of the riches of thy Son ;
act as Queen, Mother, and Spouse of the King: for
to thee belongs dominion and power over all creatures!" ‖

Mary, then is a queen : but, for our common consolation, be it known that she is a Queen so sweet,
clement, and so ready to help us in our miseries, that
the holy Church wills that we should salute her in this
prayer under the title of Queen of mercy.

"The title of queen," remarks Blessed Albert the
Great, ¶ " differs from that of empress, which implies
severity and rigor in signifying compassion and
charity towards the poor." " The greatness of kings
and queens," says Seneca, "consists in relieving the
wretched" ; ** and whereas tyrants, when they reign,
have their own good in view, kings should have that
of their subjects at heart. For this reason it is that,

---

* *De Laud. B. Virg.*   † *Ibid.*   ‡ *In Cant.* l. 3.
§ *Pro Fest. V. M.* s. 5, c. 6.   ‖ *In Ass. B. M.* s. 3.
¶ *Super Miss.* q. 162.   ** *Medea, act.* 2.

at their consecration, kings have their heads an-
nointed with oil, which is the symbol of mercy, to
denote that, as kings, they should, above all things,
nourish in their hearts feelings of compassion and
benevolence towards their subjects.

Kings should, then, occupy themselves principally
in works of mercy, but not so as to forget the just
punishments that are to be inflicted on the guilty. It
is, however, not thus with Mary, who, although a
Queen, is not a queen of justice, intent on the punishment of the wicked, but a queen of mercy, intent
only on commiserating and pardoning sinners. And
this is the reason for which the Church requires that
we should expressly call her " the Queen of mercy."
The great Chancellor of Paris, John Gerson, in his
commentary on the words of David, "These two
things have I heard, that power belongeth to God,
and mercy to Thee, O Lord," * says that the kingdom of God, consisting in justice and mercy, was
divided by Our Lord : the kingdom of justice He reserved for Himself, and that of mercy He yielded to
Mary, ordaining at the same time that all mercies
that are dispensed to men should pass through the
hands of Mary, and be disposed of by her at will.
These are Gerson's own words: " The kingdom of
God consists in power and mercy ; reserving power to
Himself, He, in some way, yielded the empire of
mercy to His Mother." † This is confirmed by St.
Thomas, in his preface to the Canonical Epistles,
saying, "that when the Blessed Virgin conceived the
Eternal Word in her womb, and brought Him forth,
she obtained half the kingdom of God; so that she is
Queen of mercy, as Jesus Christ is King of justice."

* Ps. lxi. 12. † *Super Magn.* tr. 4.

The Eternal Father made Jesus Christ the King of justice, and consequently universal Judge of the world: and therefore the Royal Prophet sings: " Give to the King Thy judgment, O God, and to the King's Son Thy justice." *   Here a learned interpreter takes up the sentence, and says: " O Lord, Thou hast given justice to Thy Son, because Thou hast given mercy to the King's Mother."   And, on this subject, St. Bonaventure, paraphrasing the words of David, thus interprets them: " Give to the King Thy judgment, O God, and Thy mercy to the Queen His Mother."   Ernest, Archbishop of Prague, also remarks, "that the Eternal Father gave the office of judge and avenger to the Son, and that of showing mercy and relieving the necessitous to the Mother."†   This was foretold by the prophet David himself; for he says that God (so to speak) consecrated Mary Queen of mercy, anointing her with the oil of gladness: " God hath anointed thee with the oil of gladness."‡   In order that we miserable children of Adam might rejoice, remembering that in heaven we have this great Queen, overflowing with the unction of mercy and compassion towards us; and thus we can say with St. Bonaventure, " O Mary, thou art full of the unction of mercy, and of the oil of compassion;" §   therefore God has anointed thee with the oil of gladness.

And how beautifully does not Blessed Albert the Great apply to this subject the history of Queen Esther, who was herself a great type of our Queen Mary!

We read, in the fourth chapter of the Book of Esther, that in the reign of Assuerus a decree was issued, by which all Jews were condemned to death. Mardochai,

* Ps. lxxi. 2.   † *Marial.* c. 127.
‡ Ps. xliv. 8.   § *Spec. B. M. V. lect.* 7.

who was one of the condemned, addressed himself to Esther, in order that she might interpose with Assuerus and obtain the revocation of the decree, and thus be the salvation of all. At first Esther declined the office, fearing that such a request might irritate the king still more; but Mardochai reproved her, sending her word that she was not to think of saving only herself, for God had placed her on the throne to obtain the salvation of all the Jews: "Think not that thou mayest save thy life only, because thou art in the king's house, more than all the Jews." * Thus did Mardochai address Queen Esther. And so can we poor sinners address our Queen Mary, should she show any repugnance to obtain of God our delivery from the chastisement we have justly deserved: "Think not, O Lady, that God has raised thee to the dignity of Queen of the world, only to provide for thy good ; but in order that, being so great, thou mightest be better able to compassionate and assist us miserable creatures."

As soon as Assuerus saw Esther standing before him, he asked her, with love, what she came to seek. "What is thy request?" The Queen replied, "If I have found favor in thy sight, O King, give me my people, for which I request."† Assuerus granted her request, and immediately ordered the revocation of the decree. And now, if Assuerus, through love for Esther, granted, at her request, salvation to the Jews, how can God refuse the prayers of Mary, loving her immensely as He does, when she prays for poor miserable sinners, who recommend themselves to her, and says to him, " My King and my God, if ever I have found favor in Thy sight " (though the divine Mother well knows that she

* Esth. iv.13.   † Esth. vii. 2, 3.

was the blessed, the holy one, the only one of the human race who found the grace lost by all mankind; well does she know that she is the beloved one of her Lord, loved more than all the saints and angels together), "give me my people for which I ask"? "If Thou lovest me", she says, "give me, O Lord, these sinners, for whom I entreat Thee." Is it possible that God should refuse her? And who is ignorant of the power of the prayers of Mary with God? "The law of clemency is on her tongue." * Each of her prayers is, as it were, an established law for Our Lord, that He should show mercy to all for whom she intercedes. St. Bernard asks why the Church calls Mary "the Queen of mercy." And he replies, that "it is because we believe that she opens the abyss of the mercy of God to whomsoever she wills, when she wills, and as she wills; so that there is no sinner, however great, who is lost if Mary protects him."†

But perhaps we may fear that Mary would not deign to interpose for some sinners, because they are so overloaded with crimes ? Or perhaps we ought to be overawed at the majesty and holiness of this great Queen ? "No," says St. Gregory VII.; "for the higher and more holy she is the greater is her sweetness and compassion towards sinners who have recourse to her with the desire to amend their lives." ‡ Kings and queens, with their ostentation of majesty, inspire terror, and cause their subjects to fear to approach them: but what fear, says St. Bernard, can the miserable have to approach this Queen of mercy for she inspires no terror, and shows no severity, to those who come to her, but is all sweetness and gentleness. "Why should

* Prov. xxxi. 26.   † *In Salve Reg.* s. i.   ‡ *Lib.* i. *Ep.* 47.

human frailty fear to go to Mary? In her there is no austerity, nothing terrible : she is all sweetness, offering milk and wool to all." * Mary is not only willing to give, but she herself offers milk and wool to all: the milk of mercy to animate our confidence, and the wool of her protection against the thunderbolts of divine justice.

Suetonius † relates of the Emperor Titus that he could never refuse a favor, so much so that he sometimes promised more than he could grant, and when admonished of this he replied, that a prince should never send away dissatisfied any person whom he admitted to his audience. Titus spoke thus, but in reality he must often have deceived or failed in his promises. Our Queen cannot deceive, and can obtain all that she wills for her clients. Moreover, "Our Lord has given her so benign and compassionate a heart," says Lanspergius, "that she cannot send away any one dissatisfied who prays to her." ‡ But how, to use the words of St. Bonaventure, canst thou, O Mary, who art the Queen of mercy, refuse to succor the miserable? And "who," asks the saint, "are the subjects for mercy if not the miserable? And since thou art the Queen of mercy," he continues, "and I am the most miserable of sinners, it follows that I am the first of thy subjects. How, then, O Lady, canst thou do otherwise than exercise thy mercy on me?"§ Have pity on us, then, O Queen of mercy, and take charge of our salvation. ·

"Say not, O holy Virgin," exclaims St. George of Nicomedia, "that thou canst not assist us on account of the number of our sins, for thy power and thy

compassion are such that no number of sins, however great, can outweigh them.   Nothing resists thy
power, for our common Creator, honoring thee as His
Mother, considers thy glory as His own;" and the Son,
" exulting in it, fulfils thy petition as if He were paying
a debt;"* meaning thereby that although Mary is
under an infinite obligation to the Son for having
chosen her to be His Mother, yet it cannot be denied
that the Son is under great obligation to her for having given Him His humanity; and therefore Jesus, to
pay, as it were, what He owes to Mary, and glorying in
her glory, honors her in a special manner by listening
to and granting all her petitions.

How great, then, should be our confidence in this
Queen, knowing her great power with God, and that
she is so rich and full of mercy that there is no one
living on the earth who does not partake of her compassion and favor.   This was revealed by our blessed
Lady herself to St. Bridget, saying, " I am the Queen
of heaven and the Mother of mercy; I am the joy of
the just, and the door through which sinners are
brought to God.   There is no sinner on earth so
accursed as to be deprived of my mercy; for all, if
they receive nothing else through my intercession, receive the grace of being less tempted by the devils
than they would otherwise have been."   " No one,"
she adds, "unless the irrevocable sentence has been
pronounced" (that is, the one pronounced on the
damned), "is so cast off by God that he will not return to Him, and enjoy His mercy, if he invokes my
aid."†   " I am called by all the Mother of mercy,
and truly the mercy of my Son towards men has made

* *Or. de Ingr. B. V.*   † Rev. l. 6, c. 10.

me thus merciful towards them ; " * and she concludes by saying, " And therefore miserable will he be, and miserable will he be to all eternity, who, in this life, having it in his power to invoke me, who am so compassionate to all, and so desirous to assist sinners, is miserable enough not to invoke me, and so is damned." †

Let us, then, have recourse, and always have recourse, to this most sweet Queen, if we would be certain of salvation; and if we are alarmed and disheartened at the sight of our sins, let us remember that it is in order to save the greatest and most abandoned sinners, who recommend themselves to her, that Mary is made the Queen of mercy. Such have to be her crown in heaven; according to the words addressed to her by her divine Spouse: " Come from Libanus, my spouse; come from Libanus, come: thou shalt be crowned ; . . . from the dens of the lions from the mountains of the leopards." ‡ And what are these dens of beasts but miserable sinners, whose souls have become the home of sin, the most frightful monster that can be found ? " With such souls," says the Abbot Rupert, addressing our blessed Lady, " saved by thy means, O great Queen Mary, wilt thou be crowned in heaven; for their salvation will form a diadem worthy of, and well-becoming, a Queen of mercy." §

* Rev. l. 2. c. 23.
† Ibid.
‡ Cant. iv. 8.
§ In Cant. l. iii.

Prayer.

O Mother of my God, and my Lady Mary; as a beggar, all wounded and sore, presents himself before a great queen, so do I present myself before thee, who art the Queen of heaven and earth. From the lofty throne on which thou sittest, disdain not, I implore thee, to cast thine eyes on me, a poor sinner. God has made thee so rich that thou mightest assist the poor, and has constituted thee Queen of Mercy in order that thou mightest relieve the miserable. Behold me then, and pity me : behold me and abandon me not, until thou seest me changed from a sinner into a saint. I know well that I merit nothing; nay more, that I deserve, on account of my ingratitude, to be deprived of the graces that, through thy means, I have already received from God. But thou, who art the Queen of Mercy, seekest not merits, but miseries, in order to help the needy. But who is more needy than I? O exalted Virgin, well do I know that thou, who art Queen of the universe, art already my queen; yet am I determined to dedicate myself more especially to thy service, in order that thou mayest dispose of me as thou pleasest. Therefore do I address thee in the words of St. Bonaventure: "Do thou govern me, O my Queen, and leave me not to myself."* Command me; employ me as thou wilt, and chastise me when I do not obey; for the chastisements that come from thy hands will be to me pledges of salvation. I would rather be thy servant than the ruler of the earth. "I am thine; save me."† Accept me, O Mary, for thine own, and as thine, take charge of my salvation. I will no longer be mine; to thee do I give myself. If, during the time past I have served thee ill, and lost so many occasions of honoring thee, for the future I will be one of thy most

---

* *Stim. div. Am.* p. 3, c. 19.   † Ps. cxviii. 94.

loving and faithful servants. I am determined that from
this day forward no one shall surpass me in honoring
and loving thee, my most amiable Queen. This I promise; and this, with thy help, I hope to execute. Amen.

II. How much our Confidence in Mary should be Increased because she is our Mother.

It is not without a meaning, or by chance, that
Mary's clients call her Mother; and indeed they seem
unable to invoke her under any other name, and
never tire of calling her Mother. Mother, yes! for
she is truly our Mother; not indeed carnally, but
spiritually; of our souls and of our salvation.

Sin, by depriving our souls of divine grace, deprived them also of life. Jesus our Redeemer, with
an excess of mercy and love, came to restore this life
by His own death on the cross, as He Himself declared: "I am come that they may have life, and
may have it more abundantly." * He says more
abundantly; for, according to theologians, the benefit of redemption far exceeded the injury done by
Adam's sin. So that by reconciling us with God He
made Himself the Father of souls in the law of grace,
as it was foretold by the prophet Isaias: "He shall
be called the Father of the world to come, the Prince
of Peace." † But if Jesus is the Father of our souls,
Mary is also their Mother; for she, by giving us Jesus,
gave us true life: and afterwards, by offering the life
of her Son on Mount Calvary for our salvation, she
brought us forth to the life of grace.

* John x. 10.   † Is. ix. 6.

On two occasions, then, according to the holy
Fathers, Mary became our spiritual Mother.

The first, according to Blessed Albert the Great,*
was when she merited to conceive in her virginal
womb the Son of God.   St. Bernardine of Siena
says the same thing more distinctly, for he tells us,
"that when at the Annunciation the most blessed
Virgin gave the consent which was expected by the
Eternal Word before becoming her Son, she from
that moment asked our salvation of God with intense
ardor, and took it to heart in such a way, that from
that moment, as a most loving mother, she bore us in
her womb." †

In the second chapter of St. Luke, the Evangelist,
speaking of the birth of our blessed Redeemer, says
that Mary " brought forth her first-born Son." ‡   Then,
remarks an author, " since the Evangelist asserts that
on this occasion the most Holy Virgin brought forth
her first-born, must we suppose that she had afterwards other children?"   But then he replies to his
own question, saying, " that as it is of faith that Mary
had no other children according to the flesh than
Jesus, she must have had other spiritual children,
and we are those children."   This was revealed by
Our Lord to St. Gertrude, § who was one day reading
the above text, and was perplexed and could not understand how Mary, being only the Mother of Jesus,
could be said to have brought forth her first-born.
God explained it to her, saying, that Jesus was Mary's
first-born according to the flesh, but that all mankind
were her second-born according to the spirit. ‖

* *De Laud. B.M.* l. 6, c. 1.
† *Pro Fest. V. M.* s. 8, a. 2, c. 2.   ‡ Luke ii. 7.
§ *Spann. Polyanth. litt. m.* t. 6.   ‖ *Insin.* l. 4, c. 3.

From what has been said, we can understand that passage of the sacred Canticles : " Thy belly is like a heap of wheat, set about with lilies," * and which applies to Mary. And it is explained by St. Ambrose, who says : " That although in the most pure womb of Mary there was but one grain of corn, which was Jesus Christ, yet it is called a heap of wheat, because all the elect were virtually contained in it ; " and as Mary was also to be their Mother, in bringing forth Jesus, He was truly and is called the first-born of many brethren.† And the Abbot St. William writes in the same sense, saying, " that Mary, in bringing forth Jesus, our Saviour and our life, brought forth many unto salvation ; and by giving birth to life itself, she gave life to many." ‡

The second occasion on which Mary became our spiritual Mother, and brought us forth to the life of grace, was when she offered to the Eternal Father the life of her beloved Son on Mount Calvary, with so bitter sorrow and suffering. So that St. Augustine declares, that " as she then cooperated by her love in the birth of the faithful to the life of grace, she became the spiritual Mother of all who are members of the one Head, Christ Jesus." § This we are given to understand by the following verse of the sacred Canticles, and which refers to the most blessed Virgin : " They have made me the keeper in the vineyards ; my vineyard I have not kept." ‖ St. William says, that " Mary, in order that she might save many souls, exposed her own to death " ; ¶ meaning, that to save us she sacrificed the life of her Son. And who but

* Cant. vii. 2. † *Ap. Novar. Umbra V.* c. 63.
‡ *Delrio, in Cant.* iv. 13. § *De S. Virginitate*, c. vi.
‖ Cant. i. 5. ¶ *Delrio, In Cant.* i. 6.

Jesus was the soul of Mary ?   He was her life, and all
her love.   And therefore the prophet Simeon foretold
that a sword of sorrow would one day transpierce her
own most blessed soul.*   And it was precisely the
lance which transpierced the side of Jesus, Who was
the soul of Mary.   Then it was that this most blessed
Virgin brought us forth by her sorrows to eternal life :
and thus we can all call ourselves the children of the
sorrows of Mary.   Our most loving Mother was always,
and in all, united to the will of God.   " And therefore," says St. Bonaventure, " when she saw the love
of the Eternal Father towards men to be so great that,
in order to save them, He willed the death of His Son ;
and, on the other hand, seeing the love of the Son in
wishing to die for us : in order to conform herself to
this excessive love of both the Father and the Son
towards the human race, she also with her entire will
offered, and consented to, the death of her Son, in
order that we might be saved." †

It is true that according to the prophecy of Isaias
Jesus, in dying for the redemption of the human race,
chose to be alone.   " I have trodden the winepress
alone " ; ‡ but, seeing the ardent desire of Mary to
aid in the salvation of man, He disposed it so that she,
by the sacrifice and offering of the life of her Jesus,
should cooperate in our salvation, and thus become
the Mother of our souls.   This Our Saviour signified,
when, before expiring, He looked down from the cross
on His Mother and on the disciple St. John, who stood
at its foot, and, first addressing Mary, He said, " Behold thy son ; " § as it were saying, Behold, the whole
human race, which by the offer thou makest of My

* Luke ii. 35.   † *In Sent.* l. i. d. 48, a. 2, q. 2.
‡ Is. lxiii. 3.   § John xix. 26.

life for the salvation of all, is even now being born to
the life of grace. Then, turning to the disciple, He
said, " Behold thy Mother." * " By these words," says
St. Bernardine of Siena, " Mary, by reason of the
love she bore them, became the Mother, not only of
St. John, but of all men." † And Silveria remarks,
that St. John himself, in stating this fact in his Gospel,
says : " Then He said to the disciple, Behold thy
Mother." Here observe well that Jesus Christ did
not address Himself to John, but to the disciple, in
order to show that He then gave Mary to all who are
His disciples, that is to say, to all Christians, that she
might be their Mother. " John is but the name of
one, whereas the word disciple is applicable to all ;
therefore Our Lord makes use of a name common to
all, to show that Mary was given as a Mother to us."‡

The Church applies to Mary these words of the sacred Canticles: " I am the Mother of fair love" ; § and
a commentator explaining them, says, that the Blessed
Virgin's love renders our souls beautiful in the sight of
God, and also makes her as a most loving mother
receive us as her children, "she being all love towards
those whom she has thus adopted." ‖ And what
mother, exclaims St. Bonaventure, loves her children,
and attends to their welfare, as thou lovest us and
carest for us, O most sweet Queen ! " For dost thou
not love us and seek our welfare far more without
comparison than any earthly mother ?" ¶

Oh, blessed are they who live under the protection of
so loving and powerful a mother ! The prophet David,
although she was not yet born, sought salvation from

* John xix. 26.   † *T.I.* s. 51, a. 1, c. 3.
‡ *In Evang.* l. viii. c. 17. q, 14.   § Ecclus. xxiv. 24.
‖ *Paciucch. In* Ps. 86, exc. 22.   ¶ *Stim. div. am.* p. 3, c. 19.

God by dedicating himself as a son of Mary, and thus
prayed : " Save the son of Thy handmaid." * Of what
handmaid ? " asks St. Augustine; and he answers, " Of
her who said, ' Behold the handmaid of the Lord.' "
" And who," says Cardinal Bellarmine, "would ever
dare to snatch these children from the bosom of Mary,
when they have taken refuge there ? What power of
hell, or what temptation, can overcome them, if they
place their confidence in the patronage of this great
Mother, the Mother of God, and of them ? " † There
are some who say that when the whale sees its young
in danger, either from tempests or pursuers, it opens
its mouth and swallows them. This is precisely what
Novarinus asserts of Mary: " When the storms of
temptation rage, the most compassionate Mother of the
faithful with maternal tenderness, protects them as it
were in her own bosom until she has brought them
into the harbor of salvation."

O most loving Mother ! O most compassionate
Mother ! be thou ever blessed; and ever blessed be
God, Who has given thee to us for our Mother, and for
a secure refuge in all the dangers of this life. Our
blessed Lady herself, in a vision, addressed these words
to St. Bridget: " As a mother, on seeing her son in the
midst of the swords of his enemies, would use every
effort to save him, so do I, and will do for all sinners
who seek my mercy." ‡ Thus it is that in every en-
gagement with the infernal powers, we shall always certainly conquer by having recourse to the Mother of
God, Who is also our Mother, saying and repeating
again and again: " We fly to thy patronage, O holy
Mother of God : we fly to thy patronage, O holy

* Ps. lxxxv. 16.
† *De Sept. Verb.* l. i. c. 12.   ‡ Rev. l. iv. cap. 138.

Mother of God." Oh, how many victories have not the faithful gained over hell, by having recourse to Mary with this short but most powerful prayer! Thus it was that the great servant of God, Sister Mary Crucified, of the Order of St. Benedict, always overcame the devils.

Be of good heart, then, all you who are children of Mary. Remember that she accepts as her children all those who choose to be so. Rejoice! Why do you fear to be lost, when such a Mother defends and protects you ? "Say, then, O my soul, with great confidence: I will rejoice and be glad; for whatever the judgment to be pronounced on me may be, it depends on and must come from my Brother and Mother."* "Thus," says St. Bonaventure, "it is that each one who loves this good Mother, and relies on her protection, should animate himself to confidence, remembering that Jesus is our Brother, and Mary our Mother." The same thought makes St. Anselm cry out with joy, and encourage us, saying : "O happy confidence! O safe refuge! the Mother of God is my Mother. How firm, then, should be our confidence, since our salvation depends on the judgment of a good Brother and a tender Mother." † It is, then, our Mother who calls us, and says, in these words of the Book of Proverbs: "He that is a little one, let him turn to me." ‡ Children have always on their lips their mother's name, and in every fear, in every danger they immediately cry out, mother! mother! Ah, most sweet Mary! ah, most loving Mother! this is precisely what thou desirest: that we should become children, and call on thee in every danger, and at all times have recourse to thee,

* *Solil.* c. 1.   † *Or.* 51.   ‡ Prov. ix. 4.

because thou desirest to help and save us, as thou hast saved all who have had recourse to thee.

Prayer.

O most holy Mother Mary, how is it possible that I, having so holy a mother, should be so wicked ? a mother all burning with the love of God, and I loving creatures ; a mother so rich in virtue, and I so poor ? Ah, amiable Mother, it is true that I do not deserve any longer to be thy son, for by my wicked life I have rendered myself unworthy of so great an honor. I am satisfied that thou shouldst accept me for thy servant; and in order to be admitted amongst the vilest of them, I am ready to renounce all the kingdoms of the world. Yes, I am satisfied. But still thou must not forbid me to call thee mother. This name consoles and fills me with tenderness, and reminds me of my obligation to love thee. This name excites me to great confidence in thee. When my sins and the divine justice fill me most with consternation, I am all consoled at the thought that thou art my mother. Allow me then to call thee mother, my most amiable mother. Thus do I call thee, and thus will I always call thee. Thou, after God, must be my hope, my refuge, my love in this valley of tears. Thus do I hope to die, breathing forth my soul into thy holy hands, and saying, My Mother, my Mother Mary, help me, have pity on me ! Amen.

III. The Greatness of the Love which this Mother bears us.

Since Mary is our Mother, we may consider how great is the love she bears us; love towards our children is a necessary impulse of nature; and St. Thomas* says that this is the reason why the divine law imposes

---

* *De Dil. Chr.* c. 13.

on children the obligation of loving their parents; but gives no express command that parents should love their children, for nature itself has so strongly implanted it in all creatures, that, as St. Ambrose remarks, "we know that a mother will expose herself to danger for her children," and even the most savage beasts cannot do otherwise than love their young.* It is said that even tigers, on hearing the cry of their cubs taken by hunters, will go into the sea and swim until they reach the vessel in which they are. Since the very tigers, says our most loving Mother Mary, cannot forget their young, how can I forget to love you, my children? And even, she adds, were such a thing possible as that a mother should forget to love her child, it is not possible that I should cease to love a soul that has become my child: "Can a woman forget her infant, so as not to have pity on the son of her womb? And if she should forget, yet will I not forget thee." †

Mary is our Mother, not, as we have already observed, according to the flesh, but by love; "I am the Mother of fair love; ‡ hence it is the love only that she bears us that makes her our mother; and therefore some one remarks "that she glories in being a mother of love, because she is all love towards us whom she has adopted for her children." § And who can ever tell the love that Mary bears us miserable creatures? Arnold of Chartres tells us that "at the death of Jesus Christ she desired with immense ardor to die with her Son, for love of us;" ‖ so much so,

---

* *Hexam.* l. 6, c. 4.

† Is. xlix. 15.   ‡ Ecclus. xxiv. 24.

§ *Paciucch. In* Ps. 86, Exc. 22.   ‖ *Ibid.* Exc. 1.

adds St. Ambrose, that whilst " her Son was hanging on the cross, Mary offered herself to the executioners," * to give her life for us.

But let us consider the reason of this love ; for then we shall be better able to understand how much this good mother loves us.

The first reason for the great love that Mary bears to men, is the great love that she bears to God ; love towards God and love towards our neighbor belong to the same commandment, as expressed by St. John : " this commandment we have from God, that he who loveth God, love also his brother ; " † so that as the one becomes greater the other also increases.   What have not the saints done for their neighbor in consequence of their love towards God !   Read only the account of the labors of St. Francis Xavier in the Indies, where, in order to aid the souls of these poor barbarians and bring them to God, he exposed himself to a thousand dangers, clambering amongst the mountains, and seeking out these poor creatures in the caves in which they dwelt like wild beasts.   See a St. Francis de Sales, who, in order to convert the heretics of the province of Chablais, risked his life every morning, for a whole year, crawling on his hands and feet over a frozen beam, in order that he might preach to them on the opposite side of a river ; a St. Paulinus, who delivered himself up as a slave, in order that he might obtain liberty for the son of a poor widow ; a St. Fidelis, who, in order to draw the heretics of a certain place to God, persisted in going to preach to them, though he knew it would cost him his life.   The saints, then, because they loved God

* *Inst. Virg.* c. 7.   † I John iv. 21.

much, did much for their neighbor ; but whoever loved God as much às Mary ? She loved Him more in the first moment of her existence than all the saints and angels ever loved Him, or will love Him ; but this we shall explain at length, when treating of her virtues. Our blessed Lady herself revealed to Sister Mary the Crucified, that the fire of love with which she was inflamed towards God was such that if the heavens and earth were placed in it they would be instantly consumed ; so that the ardors of the seraphim, in comparison with it, were but as fresh breezes. And as amongst all the blessed spirits, there is not one that loves God more than Mary, so we neither have nor can have any one who, after God, loves us as much as this most loving Mother ; and if we consecrate all the love that mothers bear their children, husbands and wives one another, all the love of angels and saints for their clients, it does not equal the love of Mary towards a single soul. Father Nieremberg* says that the love that all mothers have ever had for their children is but a shadow in comparison with the love that Mary bears to each one of us ; and he adds, that she alone loves us more than all the angels and saints put together.

Moreover, our Mother loves us much, because we were recommended to her by her beloved Jesus, when He before expiring said to her, " Woman, behold thy son ! " for we were all represented in the person of St. John, as we have already observed : these were His last words ; and the last recommendations left before death by persons we love are always treasured and never forgotten.

But again, we are exceedingly dear to Mary on ac-

---

* *De Aff. erga B. V.* c. 14.

count of the sufferings we cost her. Mothers generally love those children most, the preservation of whose life has cost them the most suffering and anxiety; we are those children for whom Mary, in order to obtain for us the life of grace, was obliged to endure the bitter agony of herself offering her beloved Jesus to die an ignominious death, and had also to see Him expire before her own eyes in the midst of the most cruel and unheard-of torments. It was then by this great offering of Mary that we were born to the life of grace; we are therefore her very dear children, since we cost her so great suffering. And thus, as it is written of the love of the Eternal Father towards men, in giving His own Son to death for us, that " God so loved the world as to give His only-begotten Son." * " So also," says St. Bonaventure, " we can say of Mary, that she has so loved us as to give her only-begotten Son for us." And when did she give Him ? She gave Him, says Father Nieremberg, when she granted Him permission to deliver Himself up to death ; she gave Him to us, when, others neglecting to do so, either out of hatred or from fear, she might herself have pleaded for the life of her Son before the judges. Well may it be supposed that the words of so wise and loving a mother would have had great weight, at least with Pilate, and might have prevented him from sentencing a man to death Whom he knew and had declared to be innocent. But no, Mary would not say a word in favor of her Son, lest she might prevent that death on which our salvation depended. Finally, she gave Him to us a thousand and a thousand times, during the three hours preced-

* John iii. 16.

ing His death, and which she spent at the foot of the
cross ; for during the whole of that time she unceasingly offered, with the extreme of sorrow and the extreme of love, the life of her Son in our behalf, and
this with such constancy, that St. Anselm and St. Antoninus say,* that if executioners had been wanting,
she herself would have crucified Him, in order to
obey the Eternal Father Who willed His death for our
salvation. If Abraham had such fortitude as to be
ready to sacrifice with his own hands the life of his
son, with far greater fortitude would Mary (far more
holy and obedient than Abraham) have sacrificed the
life of hers. But let us return to the consideration of
the gratitude we owe to Mary for so great an act of
love as was the painful sacrifice of the life of her Son,
which she made to obtain eternal salvation for us all.
God abundantly rewarded Abraham for the sacrifice
he was prepared to make of his son Isaac ; but we,
what return can we make to Mary for the life of her
Jesus, a son far more noble and beloved than the son
of Abraham ? " This love of Mary," says St. Bonaventure, " has indeed obliged us to love her ; for we
see that she has surpassed all others in love towards
us, since she has given her only Son, Whom she loved
more than herself, for us." †

From this arises another motive for the love of
Mary towards us; for in us she beholds that which has
been purchased at the price of the death of Jesus
Christ. If a mother knew that a servant had been
ransomed by a beloved son at the price of twenty
years of imprisonment and suffering, how greatly
would she esteem that servant on this account alone !
Mary well knows that her Son came into the world only

* P. 4, t. 15, c. 41, § 1. † *De B. V. M.* s. 1.

to save us poor creatures, as He Himself protested,
" I am come to save that which is lost." *   And to
save us He was pleased even to lay down His life
for us " Having become obedient unto death." † If,
then, Mary loved us but little, she would show that
she valued but little the blood of her Son, which was
the price of our salvation.   To St. Elizabeth of Hun-
gary it was revealed that Mary, from the time she
dwelt in the Temple, did nothing but pray for us,
begging that God would hasten the coming of His
Son into the world to save us.   And how much more
must we suppose that she loves us, now that she has
seen that we are valued to such a degree by her Son,
that He did not disdain to purchase us at such a cost.

Because all men have been redeemed by Jesus,
therefore Mary loves and protects them all.   It was
she who was seen by St. John in the Apocalypse,
clothed with the sun : " And a great sign appeared in
heaven : a woman clothed with the sun." ‡   She is
said to be clothed with the sun, because as there is no
one on earth who can be hidden from the heat of the
sun—" There is no one that can hide himself from
His heat" §—so there is no one living who can be
deprived of the love of Mary.   " From its heat," that
is, as blessed Raymond Jordano applies the words,
" from the love of Mary." ‖   " And who," exclaims
St. Antoninus, " can ever form an idea of the tender
care that this most loving Mother takes of all of us,"
" offering and dispensing her mercy to every one: " ¶
for our good Mother desired the salvation of all, and
cooperated in obtaining it.   " It is evident," says St.

* Luke xix. 10.   † Phil. ii. 8.
‡ Apoc. xii. 1.   § Ps. xviii. 7.
‖ *Contempl. de V. M. in prol.*
¶ P. 4, t. 15, c. 2.

Bernard, " that she was solicitous for the whole
human race." * Hence the custom of some of Mary's
clients, spoken of by Cornelius à Lapide, and which
consists in asking Our Lord to grant them the graces
that our blessed Lady seeks for them, succeeds most
advantageously. They say, Lord, grant me that which
the most blessed Virgin Mary asks for me. " And
no wonder," adds the same writer, " for our Mother
desires for us better things than we can possibly desire ourselves." The devout Bernardine de Bustis
says, that Mary " loves to do us good, and dispense
graces to us far more than we to receive them." †
On this subject Blessed Albert the Great applies to
Mary the words of the Book of Wisdom : " She preventeth them that covet her, so that she first showeth
herself unto them." ‡ Mary anticipates those who
have recourse to her by making them find her before they seek her. " The love that this good Mother
bears us is so great," says Richard of St. Laurence,
" that as soon as she perceives our want she comes
to our assistance. She comes before she is called." §

And now, if Mary is so good to all, even to the ungrateful and negligent, who love her but little, and
seldom have recourse to her, how much more loving
will she be to those who love her and often call upon
her ! " She is easily found by them that seek her." ‖
" Oh, how easy," adds the same Blessed Albert, " is it
for those who love Mary to find her, and to find her
full of compassion and love ! " In the words of the
Book of Proverbs, " I love them that love me," ¶ she
protests that she cannot do otherwise than love those
who love her. And although this most loving Lady

* *In Assumpt.* s. 4.   † *Marial,* p. 2, s. 5.
‡ Wis. vi. 14.   § *In Cant.* c. 23.
‖ Wis. vi. 13.   ¶ Prov. viii. 17.

loves all men as her children, yet, says St. Bernard, "she recognizes and loves," * that is, she loves in a more special manner, those who love her more tenderly. Blessed Raymond Jordano asserts that these happy lovers of Mary are not only loved but even served by her ; for he says that those who find the most blessed Virgin Mary, find all ; for she loves those who love her, nay more, she serves those who serve her. †

In the chronicles of the Order of St. Dominic it is related that one of the friars, named Leonard, used to recommend himself two hundred times a day to this Mother of Mercy, and that when he was attacked by his last illness he saw a most beautiful queen by his side, who thus addressed him: " Leonard, wilt thou die, and come and dwell with my Son and with me ? " " And who art thou ? " he replied. " I am," said the most blessed Virgin, for she it was, " I am the Mother of Mercy: thou hast so many times invoked me, behold, I am now come to take thee; let us go together to paradise." On the same day Leonard died, and, as we trust, followed her to the kingdom of the blessed.

" Ah, most sweet Mary ! " exclaimed the Venerable John Berchmans, of the Society of Jesus, " blessed is he who loves thee ! If I love Mary, I am certain of perseverance, and shall obtain whatever I wish from God." Therefore the devout youth was never tired of renewing his resolution, and of repeating often to himself : " I will love Mary; I will love Mary."

Oh, how much does the love of this good Mother exceed that of all her children ! Let them love her

---

* *In Salve Reg.* s. i.   † *Contempl. de V. M. in prol.*

as much as they will, Mary is always amongst lovers the most loving, says St. Ignatius the martyr.

Let them love her as did St. Stanislas Kostka, who loved this dear Mother so tenderly, that in speaking of her he moved all who heard him to love her. He had made new words and new titles with which to honor her name. He never did anything without first turning to her image to ask her blessing. When he said her office, the Rosary, or other prayers, he did so with the same external marks of affection as he would have done had he been speaking face to face with Mary; when the *Salve Regina* was sung, his whole soul, and even his whole countenance, was all inflamed with love. On being one day asked by a Father of the Society, who was going with him to visit a picture of the Blessed Virgin, how much he loved Mary,—" Father," he answered, " what more can I say? she is my mother." " But," adds the Father, " the holy youth uttered these words with such tenderness in his voice, with such an expression of countenance, and at the same time it came so fully from his heart, that it no longer seemed to be a young man, but rather an angel speaking of the love of Mary."

Let us love her as Blessed Hermann loved her. He called her the spouse of his love, for he was honored by Mary herself with this same title. Let us love her as did St. Philip Neri, who was filled with consolation at the mere thought of Mary, and therefore called her his delight. Let us love her as did St. Bonaventure, who called her not only his Lady and Mother, but to show the tenderness of his affection, even called her his heart and soul : " Hail, my Lady, my Mother; nay, even my heart, my soul ! "

Let us love her like that great lover of Mary, St. Bernard, who loved this his sweet Mother so much that he called her the ravisher of hearts ; * and to express the ardent love he bore her, added : "for hast thou not ravished my heart, O Queen ? " †

Let us call her beloved, like St. Bernardine of Siena, who daily went to visit a devotional picture of Mary, and there, in tender colloquies with his Queen, declared his love ; and when asked where he went each day he replied that he went to visit his beloved.

Let us love her as did St. Aloysius Gonzaga, whose love for Mary burnt so unceasingly, that whenever he heard the sweet name of his Mother mentioned his heart was instantly inflamed, and his countenance lighted up with a fire that was visible to all.

Let us love her as much as St. Francis Solano did, who, maddened as it were (but with a holy madness) with love for Mary, would sing before her picture, and accompany himself on a musical instrument, saying, that, like worldly lovers, he serenaded his most sweet Queen.

Finally, let us love her as so many of her servants have loved her, who never could do enough to show their love. Father John of Trexo, of the Society of Jesus, rejoiced in the name of slave of Mary; and as a mark of servitude, went often to visit her in some church dedicated in her honor. On reaching the church he poured out abundant tears of tenderness and love for Mary; then, prostrating, he licked and rubbed the pavement with his tongue and face, kissing it a thousand times, because it was the house of his beloved Lady. Father James Martinez, of the same Society, who for his devotion for our blessed

* *Ib.* † *Med. in Salve Reg.*

Lady on her feasts was carried by angels to heaven to see how they were kept there, used to say, " Would that I had the hearts of all angels and saints, to love Mary as they love her—would that I had the lives of all men, to give them all for her love ! "

Oh, that others would come to love her as did Charles, the son of St. Bridget, who said that nothing in the world consoled him so much as the knowledge that Mary was so greatly loved by God. And he added, that he would willingly endure every torment rather than allow Mary to lose the smallest degree of her glory, were such a thing possible; and that if her glory was his, he would renounce it in her favor, as being far more worthy of it.

Let us, moreover, desire to lay down our lives as a testimony of our love for Mary, as Alphonsus Rodriguez desired to do. Let us love her as did those who even cut the beloved name of Mary on their breasts with sharp instruments, as did Francis Binanzio and Radagundis, wife of King Clothaire, or as did those who could imprint this loved name on their flesh with hot irons, in order that it might remain more distinct and lasting; as did her devout servants Baptist Archinto and Augustine d'Espinosa, both of the Society of Jesus, impelled thereto by the vehemence of their love.

Let us, in fine, do or desire to do all that it is possible for a lover to do, who intends to make his affection known to the person loved. For be assured that the lovers of Mary will never be able to equal her in love. " I know, O Lady," says St. Peter Damian, " that thou art most loving, and that thou lovest us with an invincible love." * I know, my Lady, that among

* *In Nat. B. V.* s. 1.

those that love thee thou lovest the most, and that
thou lovest us with a love that can never be surpassed.

The blessed Alphonsus Rodriguez, of the Society of
Jesus, once prostrate before an image of Mary, felt his
heart inflamed with love towards this most holy Virgin, and burst forth into the following exclamation:
" My most beloved Mother, I know that thou lovest
me, but thou dost not love me as much as I love thee."
Mary, as it were offended on the point of love, immediately replied from the image : " What dost thou
say, Alphonsus—what dost thou say ? Oh, how much
greater is the love that I bear thee than any love that
thou canst have for me! Know that the distance
between heaven and earth is not so great as the distance between thy love and mine."

St. Bonaventure, then, was right in exclaiming:
Blessed are they who have the good fortune to be
faithful servants and lovers of this most loving Mother.
" Blessed are the hearts of those who love Mary;
blessed are they who are tenderly devoted to her." *
Yes ; for " in this struggle our most gracious Queen
never allows her clients to conquer her in love. She
returns our love and homage, and always increases her
past favors by new ones." † Mary, imitating in this
our most loving Redeemer Jesus Christ, returns to
those who love her their love doubled in benefits and
favors.

Then will I exclaim, with the enamoured St. Anselm, "May my heart languish and my soul melt and be
consumed with your love, O my beloved Saviour Jesus,
and my dear Mother Mary! But, as without your

---

* *Psalt. B. V. ps.* xxxi., cxviii.
† *Paciucch. in* Ps. lxxxvi. *Exc.* 2.

grace I cannot love you, grant me, O Jesus and Mary, grant my soul, by your merits and not mine, the grace to love you as you deserve to be loved. O God, lover of men, Thou couldst love guilty men even unto death. And canst Thou deny Thy love and that of Thy Mother to those who ask it?" *

Prayer.

O Lady, O ravisher of hearts! I will exclaim with St. Bonaventure: " Lady, who with the love and favor thou showest thy servants dost ravish their hearts, ravish also my miserable heart, which desires ardently to love thee. Thou, my Mother, hast enamoured a God with thy beauty, and drawn Him from heaven into thy chaste womb ; and shall I live without loving thee? " No, I will say to thee with one of thy most loving sons, John Berchmans of the Society of Jesus, I will never rest until I am certain of having obtained thy love ; but a constant and tender love towards thee, my Mother, who hast loved me with so much tenderness," even when I was ungrateful towards thee. And what should I now be, O Mary, if thou hadst not obtained so many mercies for me? Since, then, thou didst love me so much when I loved thee not, how much more may I not now hope from thee, now that I love thee? I love thee, O my Mother, and I would that I had a heart to love thee in place of all those unfortunate creatures who love thee not. I would that I could speak with a thousand tongues, that all might know thy greatness, thy holiness, thy mercy, and the love with which thou lovest all who love thee. Had I riches, I would employ them all for thy honor. Had I subjects, I would make them all thy lovers. In fine, if the occasion presented itself I would lay down my life for thy glory. I love thee, then, O my Mother ; but at the same time I fear that I do not love thee as I ought ; for I hear that love makes lovers

* *Orat.* 51.

like the person loved. If, then, I see myself so unlike thee, it is a mark that I do not love thee. Thou art so pure, and I defiled with many sins; thou so humble, and I so proud; thou so holy, and I so wicked. This, then, is what thou hast to do, O Mary; since thou lovest me, make me like thee. Thou hast all power to change hearts; take, then, mine, and change it. Show the world what thou canst do for those who love thee. Make me a saint; make me thy worthy child. This is my hope.

IV. Mary is the Mother of Penitent Sinners.

Our blessed Lady told St. Bridget that she was the mother not only of the just and innocent, but also of sinners, provided they were willing to repent.* Oh, how prompt does a sinner (desirous of amendment, and who flies to her feet) find this good Mother to embrace and help him, far more so than any earthly mother! St. Gregory VII. wrote in this sense to the princess Matilda, saying: "Resolve to sin no more, and I promise that undoubtedly thou wilt find Mary more ready to love thee than any earthly mother." †

But whoever aspires to be a child of this great mother, must first abandon sin, and then may hope to be accepted as such. Richard of St. Laurence, on the words of Proverbs, " up rose her children," ‡ remarks that the words "up rose" come first, and then the word "children," to show that no one can be a child of Mary without first endeavoring to rise from the fault into which he has fallen; for he who is in mortal sin is not worthy to be called the son of such a mother. § And St. Peter Chrysologus says that he who acts in a different manner from Mary declares

---

* Rev. l. iv. c. 138.   † *Lib.* i. ep. 47.
‡ Prov. xxxi. 28.   § *De Laud. B. V.* lib. ii. p. 5.

thereby that he will not be her son. "He who does
not the works of his mother, abjures his lineage."*
Mary humble, and he proud; Mary pure, and he
wicked; Mary full of love, and he hating his neighbor. He gives thereby proof that he is not, and will
not be, the son of his holy Mother. The sons of
Mary, says Richard of St. Laurence, are her imitators,
and this chiefly in three things: in "chastity, liberality, and humility; and also in meekness, mercy, and
such like." †

Whilst disgusting her by a wicked life, who would
dare even to wish to be the child of Mary? A certain
sinner once said to Mary, "Show thyself a Mother;"
but the Blessed Virgin replied, "Show thyself a son." ‡
Another invoked the divine Mother, calling her the
Mother of mercy, and she answered: "You sinners
when you want my help call me Mother of Mercy, and
at the same time do not cease by your sins to make
me a Mother of sorrows and anguish." § "He is
cursed of God," says Ecclesiasticus, "that angereth
his mother." ‖ "That is Mary," ¶ says Richard of St.
Laurence. God curses those who by their wicked life,
and still more by their obstinacy in sin, afflict this
tender Mother.

I say, by their obstinacy; for if a sinner, though he
may not as yet have given up his sin, endeavors to do
so, and for this purpose seeks the help of Mary, this
good Mother will not fail to assist him, and make him
recover the grace of God. And this is precisely what
St. Bridget heard one day from the lips of Jesus

* *Serm.* 123.   † *Loco cit.*
‡ *Auriem, Aff. Scamb.* p. 3, c. 12.
§ *Pelb. Stell.* l. xii. p. ult. c. 7.   ‖ Ecclus. iii. 18.
¶ *De Laud. B. M.* l. 2, p. 1.

Christ, Who, speaking to His Mother, said, " Thou
assistest him who endeavors to return to God, and
thy consolations are never wanting to any one." *   So
long, then, as a sinner is obstinate, Mary cannot love
him; but if he (finding himself chained by some
passion which keeps him a slave of hell) recommends
himself to the Blessed Virgin, and implores her, with
confidence and perseverance, to withdraw him from
the state of sin in which he is, there can be no doubt
but this good Mother will extend her powerful hand
to him, will deliver him from his chains, and lead him
to a state of salvation.

The doctrine that all prayers and works performed
in a state of sin are sins was condemned as heretical
by the sacred Council of Trent.†   St. Bernard says,‡
that although prayer in the mouth of a sinner is
devoid of beauty, as it is unaccompanied with charity,
nevertheless it is useful, and obtains grace to abandon
sin; for, as St. Thomas teaches,§ the prayer of a
sinner, though without merit, is an act which obtains
the grace of forgiveness, since the power of impetra-
tion is founded not on the merits of him who asks, but
on the divine goodness, and the merits and promises
of Jesus Christ, Who has said, " Every one that asketh
receiveth." ‖   The same thing must be said of prayers
offered to the divine Mother.   " If he who prays,"
says St. Anselm, "does not merit to be heard, the
merits of the Mother, to whom he recommends himself,
will intercede effectually." ¶

Therefore, St. Bernard exhorts all sinners to have
recourse to Mary, invoking her with great confidence;

* Rev. l. 4, c. 19.   † *Sess.* vi. *can.* 7.
‡ *De Div.* s. 81.   § 2. 2, q. 178, a. 2.
‖ Luke xi. 10.   ¶ *De Excell. Virg.* c. 6.

for though the sinner does not himself merit the graces which he asks, yet he receives them, because the Blessed Virgin asks and obtains them from God, on account of her own merits. These are His words, addressing a sinner: "Because thou wast unworthy to receive the grace thyself, it was given to Mary, in order that, through her, thou mightest receive all." *

"If a mother," continues the same saint, "knew that her two sons bore a mortal enmity to each other, and that each plotted against the other's life, would she not exert herself to her utmost in order to reconcile them? This would be the duty of a good mother. And thus it is," the saint goes on to say, "that Mary acts; for she is the Mother of Jesus, and the Mother of men. When she sees a sinner at enmity with Jesus Christ, she cannot endure it, and does all in her power to make peace between them. O happy Mary, thou art the Mother of the criminal, and the Mother of the judge; and being the Mother of both, they are thy children, and thou canst not endure discords amongst them." †

This most benign Lady only requires that the sinner should recommend himself to her, and purpose amendment. When Mary sees a sinner at her feet, imploring her mercy, she does not consider the crimes with which he is loaded, but the intention with which he comes; and if this is good, even should he have committed all possible sins, the most loving Mother embraces him, and does not disdain to heal the wounds of his soul; for she is not only called the Mother of Mercy, but is so truly and indeed, and shows herself such by the love and tenderness with which she assists

* *In Vig. Nat.* s. 3.
† *Ap. S. Bonav. Spec. B. V. lect.* 3.

us all.   And this is precisely what the Blessed Virgin
herself said to St. Bridget: "However much a man
sins, I am ready immediately to receive him when he
repents; nor do I pay attention to the number of his
sins, but only to the intention with which he comes.
I do not disdain to anoint and heal his wounds; for I
am called, and truly am, the Mother of Mercy." *

Mary is the Mother of sinners who wish to repent,
and as a mother she cannot do otherwise than compassionate them; nay more, she seems to feel, the
miseries of her poor children as if they were her own.
When the Canaanitish woman begged Our Lord to
deliver her daughter from the devil who possessed her,
she said, "Have mercy on me, O Lord, Thou Son of
David, my daughter is grievously troubled by a devil." †
But since the daughter, and not the mother, was tor-
mented, she should rather have said, "Lord, take compassion on my daughter: " and not, Have mercy on
me; but no, she said, "Have mercy on me," and she
was right; for the sufferings of children are felt by
their mother as if they were their own.   And it is
precisely thus, says Richard of St. Laurence, that
Mary prays to God when she recommends a sinner to
Him who has had recourse to her ; she cries out for
the sinful soul. "Have mercy on *me !* " " My Lord,"
she seems to say, " this poor soul that is in sin is my
daughter, and therefore, pity not so much her as me,
who am her mother." ‡

Would that all sinners had recourse to this sweet
Mother ! for then certainly all would be pardoned by
God.   "O Mary," exclaims St. Bonaventure, in rap-
turous astonishment, " thou embracest with maternal

* Rev. l. 2, c. 23.—l. 6, c. 117.
† Matt. xv. 22.   ‡ *De Laud. B. M.* l. 6.

affections a sinner despised by the whole world, nor
dost thou leave him until thou hast reconciled the
poor creature with his Judge ; " meaning that the
sinner, whilst in the state of sin, is hated and loathed
by all, even by inanimate creatures ; fire, air, and
earth would chastise him, and avenge the honor of
their outraged Lord. But if this unhappy creature
flies to Mary, will Mary reject him? Oh, no: provided he goes to her for help, and in order to amend,
she will embrace him with the affection of a mother,
and will not let him go, until, by her powerful intercession, she has reconciled him with God, and rein-
stated him in grace.

In the Second Book of Kings, we read that a wise
woman of Thecua addressed King David in the following words : " My lord, I had two sons, and for my
misfortune, one killed the other ; so that I have now
lost one, and justice demands the other, the only one
that is left; take compassion on a poor mother, and
let me not be thus deprived of both." David, moved
with compassion toward the mother, declared that the
delinquent should be set at liberty and restored to
her. Mary seems to say the same thing when God
is indignant against a sinner who has recommended
himself to her. " My God," she says, " I had two
sons, Jesus and man ; man took the life of my Jesus
on the cross, and now Thy justice would condemn the
guilty one. O Lord, my Jesus is already dead, have
pity on me, and if I have lost the one, do not make
me lose the other also."

Most certainly God will not condemn those sinners
who have recourse to Mary, and for whom she prays,
since He Himself commended them to her as her
children. The devout Lanspergius supposes Our Lord

speaking in the following terms : " I recommended all, but especially sinners, to Mary, as her children, and therefore is she so diligent and so careful in the exercise of her office, that she allows none of those committed to her charge, and especially those who invoke her, to perish ; but as far as she can, brings all to Me."   " And who can ever tell," says the devout Blosius, " the goodness, the mercy, the compassion, the love, the benignity, the clemency, the fidelity, the benevolence, the charity, of this virgin Mother towards men ?   It is such that no words can express it."

" Let us, then," says St. Bernard, " cast ourselves at the feet of this good mother, and embracing them, let us not depart until she blesses us, and thus accepts us for her children."   And who can ever doubt the compassion of this Mother ?   St. Bonaventure used to say : " Even should she take my life, I would still hope in her; and, full of confidence, would desire to die before her image, and be certain of salvation." And thus should each sinner address her when he has recourse to this compassionate Mother ; he should say:

" My Lady and Mother, on account of my sins I deserve that thou shouldst reject me, and even that thou shouldst thyself chastise me according to my deserts ; but shouldst thou reject me, or even take my life, I will still trust in thee, and hope with a firm hope that thou wilt save me.   In thee is all my confidence; only grant me the consolation of dying before thy picture, recommending myself to thy mercy, then I am convinced that I shall not be lost, but that I shall go and praise thee in heaven, in company with so many of thy servants who left this world calling on thee for help, and have all been saved by thy powerful intercession."

Prayer.

O my sovereign Queen and worthy Mother of my God, most holy Mary; I seeing myself, as I do, so despicable and loaded with so many sins, ought not to presume to call thee Mother, or even to approach thee; yet I will not allow my miseries to deprive me of the consolation and confidence that I feel in calling thee Mother; I know well that I deserve that thou shouldst reject me; but I beseech thee to remember all that thy Son Jesus has endured for me, and then reject me if thou canst. I am a wretched sinner, who, more than all others, have despised the infinite majesty of God: but the evil is done. To thee have I recourse; thou canst help me; my Mother, help me. Say not that thou canst not do so; for I know that thou art all-powerful, and that thou obtainest whatever thou desirest of God; and if thou sayest that thou wilt not help me, tell me at least to whom I can apply in this my so great misfortune. "Either pity me," will I say with the devout St. Anselm, "O my Jesus, and forgive me, and do thou pity me, my Mother Mary, by interceding for me, or at least tell me to whom I can have recourse, who is more compassionate, or in whom I can have greater confidence than in thee." Oh, no; neither on earth nor in heaven can I find any one who has more compassion for the miserable, or who is better able to assist me, than thou canst, O Mary. Thou, O Jesus, art my Father, and thou, Mary, art my Mother. You both love the most miserable, and go seeking them in order to save them. I deserve hell, and am the most miserable of all. But you need not seek me, nor do I presume to ask so much. I now present myself before you with a certain hope that I shall not be abandoned. Behold me at your feet; **my Jesus, forgive me; my Mother Mary, help me.**

CHAPTER II.

Vita, Dulcedo.

OUR LIFE, OUR SWEETNESS.

MARY, OUR LIFE, OUR SWEETNESS.

I. Mary is our Life, because she Obtains for us the Pardon of our Sins.

To understand why the holy Church makes us call Mary our life we must know, that as the soul gives life to the body so does divine grace give life to the soul; for a soul without grace has the name of being alive, but is in truth dead, as it was said of one in the Apocalypse, "Thou hast the name of being alive, and thou art dead."* Mary, then, in obtaining this grace for sinners by her intercession, thus restores them to life.

See how the Church makes her speak, applying to her the following words of Proverbs: "They that in the morning early watch for me shall find me."† They who are diligent in having recourse to me in the morning, that is, as soon as they can, will most certainly find me. In the Septuagint the words "shall find me" are rendered "shall find grace." So that to have recourse to Mary is the same thing as to find the grace of God. A little further on she says, "He that shall find me shall find life, and shall have salvation

* Apoc. iii. 1.　　　　　† Prov. viii. 17.

from the Lord." "Listen," exclaims St. Bonaventure
on these words, "listen, all you who desire the kingdom of God; honor the most blessed Virgin Mary
and you will find life and eternal salvation." *

St. Bernardine of Siena says, that if God did not
destroy man after his first sin, it was on account of
His singular love for this holy Virgin, who was destined to be born of this race. And the saint adds,
"that he has no doubt but that all the mercies granted
by God under the Old Dispensation were granted only
in consideration of this most blessed Lady." †

Hence St. Bernard was right in exhorting us "to
seek for grace, and to seek it by Mary"; ‡ meaning,
that if we have had the misfortune to lose the grace of
God, we should seek to recover it, but we should do
so through Mary; for though we may have lost it, she
has found it; and hence the saint calls her " the finder
of grace." § The angel Gabriel expressly declared this
for our consolation, when he saluted the Blessed Vir-
gin saying " Fear not, Mary, thou hast found grace." ||
But if Mary had never been deprived of grace, how
could the archangel say that she had then found it ?
A thing may be found by a person who did not pre-
viously possess it; but we are told by the same archangel that the Blessed Virgin was always with God,
always in grace, nay, full of grace. "Hail, full of
grace, the Lord is with thee." Since Mary, then, did
not find grace for herself, she being always full of it,
for whom did she find it ? Cardinal Hugo, in his commentary on the above text, replies that she found it for
sinners who had lost it. " Let sinners, then," says this
devout writer, " who by their crimes have lost grace,

* *Psalt. B. V. ps.* 48. † *Pro Fest. V. M.* s. 5, c. 2.
‡ *De Aquæd.* § *In. Adv. D.* s. 2. || Luke i. 30.

address themselves to the Blessed Virgin, for with her they will surely find it; let them humbly salute her, and say with confidence, " Lady, that which has been found must be restored to him who has lost it; restore us, therefore, our property which thou hast found." On this subject, Richard of St. Laurence concludes, " that if we hope to receive the grace of God, we must go to Mary, who has found it, and finds it always." * And as she always was and always will be dear to God, if we have recourse to her we shall certainly succeed.

Again, Mary says, in the eighth chapter of the sacred Canticles, that God has placed her in the world to be our defence: " I am a wall: and my breasts are as a tower." † And she is truly made a mediatress of peace between sinners and God; " Since I am become in His presence as one finding peace." On these words St. Bernard encourages sinners, saying, " Go to this Mother of Mercy, and show her the wounds which thy sins have left on thy soul; then will she certainly entreat her Son, by the breasts that gave Him suck, to pardon thee all. And this divine Son, Who loves her so tenderly, will most certainly grant her petition." In this sense it is that the holy Church, in her almost daily prayer, calls upon us to beg Our Lord to grant us the powerful help of the intercession of Mary to rise from our sins: " Grant Thy help to our weakness, O most merciful God; and that we who are mindful of the holy Mother of God, may by the help of her intercession rise from our iniquities."

With reason, then, does St. Laurence Justinian call her " the hope of malefactors," ‡ since she alone is the one who obtains them pardon from God. With

---

* *De Laud. V.* 1. 2, p. 5.   † Cant. viii. 10.
‡ *S. de Nat. V. M.*

reason does St. Bernard call her "the sinners' ladder," * since she, the most compassionate Queen, extending her hand to them, draws them from an abyss of sin, and enables them to ascend to God. With reason does an ancient writer call her "the only hope of sinners," for by her help alone can we hope for the remission of our sins.†

St. John Chrysostom also says "that sinners receive pardon by the intercession of Mary alone." And therefore the saint, in the name of all sinners, thus addresses her : " Hail, Mother of God and of us all, 'heaven,' where God dwells, 'throne,' from which our Lord dispenses all grace, 'fair daughter, Virgin, honor, glory, and firmament of our Church,' assiduously pray to Jesus that in the day of judgment we may find mercy through thee, and receive the reward prepared by God for those who love Him." ‡

With reason, finally, is Mary called, in the words of the sacred Canticles, the dawn : "Who is she that cometh forth as the morning rising ?" § Yes, says Pope Innocent III., "for as the dawn is the end of night, and the beginning of day, well may the Blessed Virgin Mary, who was the end of vices, be called the dawn of day." ‖ When devotion towards Mary begins in a soul it produces the same effect that the birth of this most holy Virgin produced in the world. It puts an end to the night of sin, and leads the soul into the path of virtue. Therefore, St. Germanus says, " O Mother of God, thy protection never ceases, thy intercession is life, and thy patronage never fails." ¶ And in a sermon the same saint says, that to pronounce the name

---

* *De Aquæd.*   † *Serm.* 194, *E. B. app.*
‡ *Off. B. M. lect.* 6.   § Cant. vi. 9.
‖ *In Assumpt.* s. 2.   ¶ *In Dorm. B. V.* s. 2.

of Mary with affection is a sign of life in the soul, or
at least that life will soon return there.

We read in the Gospel of St. Luke that Mary said,
" Behold, from henceforth all generations shall call
me blessed." * " Yes, my Lady," exclaims St. Bernard, " all generations shall call thee blessed, for thou
hast begotten life and glory for all generations of
men." † For this cause all men shall call thee blessed,
for all thy servants obtain through thee the life of
grace and eternal glory. " In thee do sinners find
pardon, and the just perseverance and eternal life." ‡
" Distrust not, O sinner," says the devout Bernardine
de Bustis, " even if thou hast committed all possible
sins : go with confidence to this most glorious Lady,
and thou wilt find her hands filled with mercy and
bounty." And, he adds, for " she desires more to do
thee good than thou canst desire to receive favors
from her." §

St. Andrew of Crete calls Mary the pledge of divine
mercy ; ‖ meaning that, when sinners have recourse to
Mary, that they may be reconciled with God, He assures them of pardon and gives them a pledge of it ;
and this pledge is Mary, whom He has bestowed upon
us for our advocate, and by whose intercession (by
virtue of the merits of Jesus Christ) God forgives all
who have recourse to her. St. Bridget heard an angel
say, that the holy prophets rejoiced in knowing that
God, by the humility and purity of Mary, was to be
reconciled with sinners, and to receive those who had
offended Him to favor. " They exulted, foreknowing
that Our Lord Himself would be appeased by thy
humility, and the purity of thy life, O Mary, thou

* Luke i. 48.   † *In Pentec.*   ‡ *In Pentec.* s. 2.
§ *Marial.* p. 2, s. 5.   ‖ *In Dorm. B. V.* s. 3.

supereffulgent star, and that He would be reconciled with those who had provoked His wrath." *

No sinner having recourse to the compassion of Mary should fear being rejected ; for she is the Mother of Mercy, and as such desires to save the most miserable. Mary is that happy ark, says St. Bernard, " in which those who take refuge will never suffer the shipwreck of eternal perdition." † At the time of the deluge even brutes were saved in Noe's ark. Under the mantle of Mary even sinners obtain salvation. St. Gertrude once saw Mary with her mantle extended, and under it many wild beasts—lions, bears, and tigers —had taken refuge.‡ And she remarked that Mary not only did not reject, but even welcomed and caressed, them with the greatest tenderness. The saint understood hereby that the most abandoned sinners who have recourse to Mary are not only not rejected, but that they are welcomed and saved by her from eternal death. Let us, then, enter this ark, let us take refuge under the mantle of Mary, and she most certainly will not reject us, but will secure our salvation.

Prayer.

Behold, O Mother of my God, my only hope, Mary, behold at thy feet a miserable sinner, who asks thee for mercy. Thou art proclaimed and called by the whole Church, and by all the faithful, the refuge of sinners. Thou art consequently my refuge ; thou hast to save me. I will say with William of Paris : Thou knowest, most sweet Mother of God, how much thy blessed Son desires our salvation.§ Thou knowest all that Jesus Christ endured for this end. I present thee, O my Mother, the

---

* *Serm. Ang.* c. 9.   † *S. de B. V. M. Deip.*
‡ *Insin.* l. 4, c. 50.   § *Rhet. Div.* c. 18.

sufferings of Jesus : the cold that He endured in the stable, His journey into Egypt, His toils, His sweat, the blood that He shed ; the anguish which caused His death on the cross, and of which thou wast thyself a witness. Oh, show that thou lovest thy beloved Son, and by this love I implore thee to assist me. Extend thy hand to a poor creature who has fallen and asks thy help. Were I a saint I would not need seek thy mercy ; but because I am a sinner I fly to thee, who art the Mother of mercies. I know that thy compassionate heart finds its consolation in assisting the miserable, when thou canst do so, and dost not find them obstinate. Console, then, thy compassionate heart, and console me this day ; for now thou hast the opportunity of saving a poor creature condemned to hell ; and thou canst do so, for I will not be obstinate. I abandon myself into thy hands, only tell me what thou wouldst have me do, and obtain for me strength to execute it, for I am resolved to do all that depends on me to recover the divine grace. I take refuge under thy mantle. Jesus wills that I should have recourse to thee, in order not only that His blood may save me, but also that thy prayers may assist me in this great work ; for thy glory, and for His own, since thou art His Mother. He sends me to thee, that thou mayst help me. O Mary, see, I have recourse to thee; in thee do I confide. Thou prayest for so many others, pray also for me ; say only a word. Tell Our Lord that thou willest my salvation, and God will certainly save me. Say that I am thine, and then I have obtained all that I ask, all that I desire.

II. Mary is also our Life, because she Obtains for us Perseverance.

Final perseverance is so great a gift of God, that (as it was declared by the holy Council of Trent) it is quite gratuitous on His part, and we cannot *merit* it. Yet we are told by St. Augustine, that all who seek for it obtain it from God; and, according to Father Suarez, they obtain it infallibly, if only they are diligent in asking for it to the end of their lives. For, as Bellarmine well remarks, " that which is daily required must be asked for every day." Now, if it is true (and I hold it as certain, according to the now generally received opinion, and which I shall prove in the fourth chapter of this work) that all the graces that God dispenses to men pass through the hands of Mary, it will be equally true that it is only through Mary that we can hope for this greatest of all graces —perseverance. And we shall obtain it most certainly if we always seek it with confidence through Mary. This grace she herself promises to all who serve her faithfully during life, in the following words of Ecclesiasticus, and which are applied to her by the Church, * on the feast of her Immaculate Conception: " They that work by me shall not sin. They that explain me shall have life everlasting." †

In order that we may be preserved in the life of grace, we require spiritual fortitude to resist the many enemies of our salvation. Now this fortitude can be obtained only by the means of Mary, and we are assured of it in the Book of Proverbs, for the Church applies the passage to this most blessed Virgin.

* *Off. Imm. Conc.* † Ecclus. xxiv. 30.

"Strength is mine; by me kings reign;"* meaning by the words "strength is mine" that God has bestowed this precious gift on Mary, in order that she may dispense it to her faithful clients. And by the words "by me kings reign" she signifies that by her means her servants reign over and command their senses and passions, and thus become worthy to reign eternally in heaven. Oh, what strength do the servants of this great Lady possess to overcome all the assaults of hell! Mary is that tower spoken of in the sacred Canticles: "Thy neck is as the tower of David, which is built with bulwarks; a thousand bucklers hang upon it, all the armor of valiant men." † She is as a well-defended fortress in defence of her lovers, who in their wars have recourse to her. In her do her clients find all shields and arms to defend themselves against hell.

And for the same reason the most blessed Virgin is called a plane-tree in the words of Ecclesiasticus: "As a plane-tree by the water in the streets was I exalted." ‡ Cardinal Hugo explains them, and says that the "plane-tree has leaves like shields," to show how Mary defends all who take refuge with her. Blessed Amedeus gives another explanation, and says that this holy Virgin is called a plane-tree because, as the plane shelters travellers under its branches from the heat of the sun and from the rain, so do men find refuge under the mantle of Mary from the ardor of their passions and from the fury of temptations.§ Truly are those souls to be pitied who abandon this defence, in ceasing their devotion to Mary, and no longer recommending themselves to her in the time of dan-

---

* Prov. viii. 14.—*Off. B. V.*　　† Cant. iv. 4.

‡ Ecclus. xxiv. 19.　　§ *De Laud. B. V. hom.* 8.

ger. If the sun ceased to rise, says St. Bernard, how could the world become other than a chaos of darkness and horror? And applying this question to Mary, he repeats it. " Take away the sun, and where will be the day? Take away Mary, and what will be left but the darkest night?" * When a soul loses devotion to Mary it is immediately enveloped in darkness, and in that darkness of which the Holy Ghost speaks in the Psalms: " Thou hast appointed darkness, and it is night; in it shall all the beasts of the woods go about." † When the light of heaven ceases to shine in a soul, all is darkness, and it becomes the haunt of devils and of every sin. St. Anselm says, that " if any one is disregarded and condemned by Mary, he is necessarily lost," and therefore we may with reason exclaim, " Woe to those who are in opposition to this sun !" Woe to those who despise its light ! that is to say, all who despise devotion to Mary.

St. Francis Borgia always doubted the perseverance of those in whom he did not find particular devotion to the Blessed Virgin. On one occasion he questioned some novices as to the saints towards whom they had special devotion, and perceiving some who had it not towards Mary, he instantly warned the master of novices, and desired him to keep a more attentive watch over these unfortunate young men, who all, as he had feared, lost their vocation and renounced the religious state.

It was, then, not without reason that St. Germanus called the most blessed Virgin the breath of Christians; for as the body cannot live without breathing,

* *De Aquæd.* † Ps. ciii. 20.

so the soul cannot live without having recourse to
and recommending itself to Mary, by whose means we
certainly acquire and preserve the life of divine grace
within our souls.   But I will quote the saint's own
words: " As breathing is not only a sign but even a
cause of life, so the name of Mary, which is constantly found on the lips of God's servants, both
proves that they are truly alive, and at the same time
causes and preserves their life, and gives them every
succor." *

Blessed Allan was one day assaulted by a violent
temptation, and was on the point of yielding, for he
had not recommended himself to Mary, when the
most blessed Virgin appeared to him; and in order
that another time he might remember to invoke her
aid, she gave him a blow, saying, " If thou hadst
recommended thyself to me, thou wouldst not have
run into such danger."

On the other hand, Mary says in the following
words of the Book of Proverbs, which are applied to
her by the Church : " Blessed is the man that heareth
me, and that watcheth daily at my gates, and waiteth
at the posts of my doors," †—as if she would say,
Blessed is he that hears my voice and is constantly attentive to apply at the door of my mercy, and seeks
light and help from me.   For clients who do this
Mary does her part, and obtains them the light and
strength they require to abandon sin and walk in the
paths of virtue.   For this reason Innocent III. beautifully calls her " the moon at night, the dawn at break
of day, and the sun at midday." ‡   She is a moon to
enlighten those who blindly wander in the night of

* *De Zona Deip.*   † Prov. viii. 34.—*Off. B. V.*
‡ *In Assumpt.* s. 2.

sin, and makes them see and understand the miserable
state of damnation in which they are ; she is the dawn
(that is, the forerunner of the sun) to those whom she
has already enlightened, and makes them abandon sin
and return to God, the true sun of justice ; finally, she
is a sun to those who are in a state of grace, and prevents them from again falling into the precipice of
sin.

Learned writers apply the following words of Ecclesiasticus to Mary : " Her bands are a healthful binding."* "Why bands," asks St. Laurence Justinian,
"except it be that she binds her servants, and thus
prevents them from straying into the paths of vice ?"†
And truly this is the reason for which Mary binds her
servants. St. Bonaventure also, in his commentary
on the words of Ecclesiasticus, frequently used in the
office of Mary, " My abode is in the full assembly of
saints,"‡ says that Mary not only has her abode in
the full assembly of saints, but also preserves them
from falling, keeps a constant watch over their virtue,
that it may not fail, and restrains the evil spirits from
injuring them.   Not only has she her abode in the
full assembly of the saints, but she keeps the saints
there, by preserving their merits, that they may not
lose them, by restraining the devils from injuring them,
and by withholding the arm of her Son from falling
on sinners. §

In the Book of Proverbs we are told that all Mary's
clients are clothed with double garments. "For all
her domestics are clothed with double garments." ‖
Cornelius à Lapide explains what this double clothing

---

* Ecclus. vi. 31.   † *De Laud. B. M.* l. 2, p. 3.
‡ Ecclus. xxiv. 16.   § *Spec. B. V. M. lect.* 7.
‖ Prov. xxxi. 21.

is : he says that it " consists in her adorning her faithful servants with the virtues of her Son and with her own," and thus clothed they persevere in virtue.

Therefore St. Philip Neri, in his exhortations to his penitents, used always to say : " My children. if you desire perseverance, be devout to our blessed Lady." The Venerable John Berchmans, of the Society of Jesus, used also to say : " Whoever loves Mary will have perseverance." Truly beautiful is the reflection of the Abbot Rupert on this subject in his commentary on the parable of the prodigal son. He says, " That if this dissolute youth had had a mother living, he would never have abandoned the paternal roof, or at least would have returned much sooner than he did ; " meaning thereby that a son of Mary either never abandons God, or, if he has this misfortune, by her help he soon returns.

Oh, did all men but love this most benign and loving Lady, had they but recourse to her always, and without delay, in their temptations, who would fall ? who would ever be lost ? He falls and is lost who has not recourse to Mary. St. Laurence Justinian applies to Mary the words of Ecclesiasticus, " I have walked in the waves of the sea ; " * and makes her say, " I walk with my servants in the midst of the tempests to which they are constantly exposed, to assist and preserve them from falling into sin." †

Bernardine de Bustis relates that a bird was taught to say, " Hail, Mary ! " A hawk was on the point of seizing it, when the bird cried out, " Hail, Mary ! " In an instant the hawk fell dead. God intended to show thereby that if even an irrational creature was pre-

* Ecclus. xxiv. 8. † *De Laud. B. M.* l. 2, p. 1.

served by calling on Mary, how much more would those who are prompt in calling on her when assaulted by devils be delivered from them. We, says St. Thomas of Villanova, need only, when tempted by the devil, imitate little chickens, which, as soon as they perceive the approach of a bird of prey, run under the wings of their mother for protection. This is exactly what we should do whenever we are assaulted by temptation: we should not stay to reason with it, but immediately fly and place ourselves under the mantle of Mary. I will, however, quote the saint's own words addressed to Mary: "As chickens when they see a kite soaring above run and find refuge under the wings of the hen, so are we preserved under the shadow of thy wings. And thou," he continues, "who art our Lady and Mother, hast to defend us; for after God we have no other refuge than thee, who art our only hope and our protectress; towards thee we all turn our eyes with confidence."

Let us, then, conclude in the words of St. Bernard: "O man, whoever thou art, understand that in this world thou art tossed about on a stormy and tempestuous sea, rather than walking on solid ground; remember that if thou wouldst avoid being drowned thou must never turn thine eyes from the brightness of this star, but keep them fixed on it, and call on Mary. In dangers, in straits, in doubts, remember Mary, invoke Mary." Yes, in dangers of sinning, when molested by temptations, when doubtful as to how you should act, remember that Mary can help you; and call upon her, and she will instantly succor you. "Let not her name leave thy lips, let it be ever in thy heart." Your hearts should never lose confidence in her holy name, nor should your lips ever cease to invoke it. "Following her, thou wilt certainly not go astray." Oh, no, if we follow Mary, we shall never err from the paths of salvation. "Imploring her, thou wilt not despair." Each time that we invoke her aid, we shall be inspired with perfect confidence. "If she supports thee, thou canst not fall;" "if she protects thee, thou hast nothing to fear, for thou canst not be lost;" "with her for thy guide, thou wilt not be weary, for thy salvation will be worked out with ease." "If she is propitious, thou wilt gain the port." If Mary undertakes our defence we are certain of gaining the kingdom of heaven. "This do, and thou shalt live."

Prayer.

O compassionate Mother, most sacred Virgin, behold at thy feet the traitor, who, by paying with ingratitude the graces received from God through thy means, has betrayed both thee and Him. But I must tell thee, O most blessed Lady, that my misery, far from taking away my confidence, increases it; for I see that thy compassion is great in proportion to the greatness of my misery. Show thyself, O Mary, full of liberality towards me; for thus thou art towards all who invoke thy aid. All that I ask is that thou shouldst cast thine eyes of compassion on me, and pity me. If thy heart is thus far moved, it cannot do otherwise than protect me; and if thou protectest me, what can I fear? No, I fear nothing, I do not fear my sins, for thou canst provide a remedy; I do not fear devils, for thou art more powerful than the whole of hell; I do not even fear thy Son, though justly irritated against me, for at a word of thine He will be appeased. I only fear lest, in my temptations, and by my own fault, I may cease to recommend myself to thee, and thus be lost. But I now promise thee that I will always have recourse to thee; oh, help me to fulfil my promise. Lose not the opportunity which now presents itself of gratifying thy ardent desire to succor such poor wretches as myself. In thee, O Mother of God, I have unbounded confidence. From thee I hope for grace to bewail my sins as I ought, and from thee I hope for strength never again to fall into them. If I am sick, thou, O heavenly physician, canst heal me. If my sins have weakened me, thy help will strengthen me. O Mary, I hope all from thee; for thou art all-powerful with God. Amen.

III. Mary our Sweetness; she renders Death sweet to her Clients.

"He that is a friend loveth at all times; and a brother is proved in distress," * says the Book of Proverbs. We can never know our friends and relatives in the time of prosperity; it is only in the time of adversity that we see them in their true colors. People of the world never abandon a friend as long as he is in prosperity; but should misfortunes overtake him, and more particularly should he be at the point of death, they immediately forsake him. Mary does not act thus with her clients. In their afflictions, and more particularly in the sorrows of death, the greatest that can be endured in this world, this good Lady and Mother not only does not abandon her faithful servants, but as during our exile she is our life, so also is she at our last hour our sweetness, by obtaining for us a calm and happy death. For from the day on which Mary had the privilege and sorrow of being present at the death of Jesus her Son, Who was the head of all the predestined, it became her privilege to assist also at their deaths. And for this reason the holy Church teaches us to beg this most blessed Virgin to assist us, especially at the moment of death: "Pray for us, sinners, now and at the hour of our death!"

* Prov. xvii. 17.

Oh, how great are the sufferings of the dying ! They suffer from remorse of conscience on account of past sins, from fear of the approaching judgment, and from the uncertainty of their eternal salvation. Then it is that hell arms itself, and spares no efforts to gain the soul which is on the point of entering eternity; for it knows that only a short time remains in which to gain it, and that if it then loses it it has lost it forever. "The devil is come down unto you, having great wrath, knowing that he hath but a short time."* And for this reason the enemy of our salvation, whose charge it was to tempt the soul during life, does not choose at death to be alone, but calls others to his assistance, according to the prophet Isaias: "Their houses shall be filled with serpents."† And indeed they are so; for when a person is at the point of death, the whole place in which he is is filled with devils, who all unite to make him lose his soul.

It is related of St. Andrew Avellino that ten thousand devils came to tempt him at his death. The conflict that he had in his agony with the powers of hell was so terrible that all the good religious who assisted him trembled. They saw the saint's face swelled to such a degree from agitation that it became quite black, every limb trembled and was contorted; his eyes shed a torrent of tears, his head shook violently; all gave evidence of the terrible assault he was enduring on the part of his infernal foes. All wept with compassion, and redoubled their prayers, and at the same time trembled with fear on seeing a saint die thus. They were, however, consoled at seeing that often, as if seeking for help, the saint turned his eyes

* Apoc. xii. 12.　　　　　　　　† Is. xiii. 21.

towards a devout picture of Mary; for they remembered that during life he had often said that at death Mary would be his refuge. At length God was pleased to put an end to the contest by granting him a glorious victory; for the contortions of his body ceased, his face resumed its original size and color, and the saint, with his eyes tranquilly fixed on the picture, made a devout inclination to Mary (who it is believed then appeared to him), as if in the act of thanking her, and with a heavenly smile on his countenance tranquilly breathed forth his blessed soul into the arms of Mary. At the same moment a Capuchiness, who was in her agony, turning to the nuns who surrounded her, said, " Recite a Hail Mary; for a saint has just expired."

Ah, how quickly do the rebellious spirits fly from the presence of this Queen! If at the hour of death we have only the protection of Mary, what need we fear from all our infernal enemies? David, fearing the horrors of death, encouraged himself by placing his reliance on the death of the coming Redeemer and on the intercession of the virgin Mother. " For though," he says, " I should walk in the midst of the shadow of death, . . . Thy rod and Thy staff, they have comforted me." * Cardinal Hugo, explaining these words of the Royal Prophet, says that the staff signifies the cross, and the rod is the intercession of Mary; for she is the rod foretold by the prophet Isaias: " And there shall come forth a rod out of the root of Jesse, and a flower shall rise up out of his root." † " This divine Mother," says St. Peter Damian, " is that powerful rod with which the violence of the infernal enemies is conquered." ‡ And therefore does St. Antoninus en-

---

courage us, saying, " If Mary is for us, who shall be against us ? "

When Father Emanuel Padial, of the Society of Jesus, was at the point of death, Mary appeared to him, and to console him she said: " See at length the hour is come when the angels congratulate thee, and exclaim: O happy labors, O mortifications well requited! And in the same moment an army of demons was seen taking its flight, and crying out in despair : Alas! we can do naught, for she who is without stain defends him." In like manner, Father Gaspar Haywood was assaulted by devils at his death, and greatly tempted against faith; he immediately recommended himself to the most blessed Virgin, and was heard to exclaim, " I thank thee, Mary; for thou hast come to my aid."*

St. Bonaventure tells us that Mary sends without delay the prince of the heavenly court, St. Michael, with all the angels, to defend her dying servants against the temptations of the devils, and to receive the souls of all who in a special manner and perseveringly have recommended themselves to her. The saint, addressing our blessed Lady, says, " Michael, the leader and prince of the heavenly army, with all the administering spirits, obeys thy commands, O Virgin, and defends and receives the souls of the faithful who have particularly recommended themselves to thee, O Lady, day and night."†

The prophet Isaias tells us that when a man is on the point of leaving the world hell is opened and sends forth its most terrible demons, both to tempt the soul before it leaves the body, and also to accuse

* *Menol.* 28 *Apr.*–9 *Jan.*   † *Spec. B. V. lect.* 3.

it when presented before the tribunal of Jesus Christ for judgment. The prophet says, " Hell below was in an uproar to meet thee at thy coming; it stirred up the giants for thee." * But Richard of St. Laurence remarks that when the soul is defended by Mary the devils dare not even accuse it, knowing that the Judge never condemned, and never will condemn, a soul protected by His august Mother. He asks, " Who would dare accuse one who is patronized by the Mother of Him Who is to judge ? " † Mary not only assists her beloved servants at death and encourages them, but she herself accompanies them to the tribunal seat of God.

As St. Jerome says, writing to the virgin Eustochia, " What a day of joy will that be for thee, when Mary the Mother of Our Lord, accompanied by choirs of virgins, will go to meet thee." ‡ The Blessed Virgin assured St. Bridget of this; for, speaking of her devout clients at the point of death, she said, " Then will I, their dear Lady and Mother, fly to them, that they may have consolation and refreshment." § St. Vincent Ferrer says, that not only does the most blessed Virgin console and refresh them, but that " she receives the souls of the dying." This loving Queen takes them under her mantle, and thus presents them to the Judge, her Son, and most certainly obtains their salvation. This really happened to Charles, the son of St. Bridget,‖ who died in the army, far from his mother. She feared much for his salvation on account of the dangers to which young men are exposed in a military career; but the Blessed Virgin revealed to her that he was saved on account of his love for

* Is. xiv. 9.   † *De Laud. V.* l. 2, p. 1.
‡ *De Cust. virg.*   § Rev. l. 1, c. 29.   ‖ Rev. l. 7, c. 13.

her, and that in consequence she herself had assisted
him at death, and had suggested to him the acts that
should be made at that terrible moment.   At the same
time the saint saw Jesus on His throne, and the devil
bringing two accusations against the most blessed Virgin: the first was, that Mary had prevented him from
tempting Charles at the moment of death; and the
second was, that the Blessed Virgin had herself presented his soul to the Judge, and so saved it without
even giving him the opportunity of exposing the
grounds on which he claimed it.   She then saw the
Judge drive the devil away, and Charles's soul carried
to heaven.

Ecclesiasticus says, that "her bands are a healthful
binding," * and that "in the latter end thou shalt find
rest in her." †   Oh, you are indeed fortunate, my
brother, if at death you are bound with the sweet
chains of the love of the Mother of God !   These
chains are chains of salvation; they are chains that
will insure your eternal salvation, and will make you
enjoy in death that blessed peace which will be the
beginning of your eternal peace and rest.   Father
Binetti, in his book on the perfections of our blessed
Lord, says, "that having attended the death-bed of a
great lover of Mary, he heard him, before expiring,
utter these words: 'O my father, would that you
could know the happiness that I now enjoy from having served the most holy Mother of God; I cannot
tell you the joy that I now experience.'" ‡   Father
Suarez (in consequence of his devotion to Mary,
which was such that he used to say that he would
willingly exchange all his learning for the merit of a

single " Hail Mary ") died with such peace and joy that in that moment he said, " I could not have thought that death was so sweet;" meaning, that he could never have imagined that it was possible, if he had not then experienced it, that he could have found such sweetness in death.

You, devout reader, will, without doubt, experience the same joy and contentment in death if you can then remember that you have loved this good Mother, who cannot be otherwise than faithful to her children who have been faithful in serving and honoring her, by their visits, rosaries, and fasts, and still more by frequently thanking and praising her, and often recommending themselves to her powerful protection. Nor will this consolation be withheld, even if you have been for a time a sinner, provided that, from this day, you are careful to live well, and to serve this most gracious and benign Lady. In your pains, and in the temptations to despair which the devil will send you, she will console you, and even come herself to assist you in your last moments. St. Peter Damian relates* that his brother Martin had one day offended God grievously. Martin went before an altar of Mary, to dedicate himself to her as her slave; and for this purpose, and as a mark of servitude, put his girdle round his neck, and thus addressed her: " My sovereign Lady, mirror of that purity which I, miserable sinner that I am, have violated, thereby outraging my God and thee, I know no better remedy for my crime than to offer myself to thee for thy slave. Behold me then: to thee do I this day dedicate myself, that I may be thy servant; accept me, though a rebel, and reject me

* *De Bono Suffr.* c. 4.

not." He then left a sum of money on the step of the altar, and promised to pay a like sum every year, as a tribute which he owed as a slave of Mary. After a certain time Martin fell dangerously ill; but one morning, before expiring, he was heard to exclaim: "Rise, rise, pay homage to my Queen!" and then he added: "And whence is this favor, O Queen of heaven, that thou shouldst condescend to visit thy poor servant? Bless me, O Lady, and permit me not to be lost, after having honored me with thy presence." At this moment his brother Peter entered, and to him he related the visit of Mary, and added that she had blessed him, but at the same time complained that those who were present had remained seated in the presence of this great Queen; and shortly afterwards he sweetly expired in Our Lord.

Such also will be your death, beloved reader, if you are faithful to Mary. Though you may have hitherto offended God, she will procure you a sweet and happy death. And if by chance at that moment you are greatly alarmed and lose confidence at the sight of your sins, she will come and encourage you, as she did Adolphus, Count of Alsace, who abandoned the world, and embraced the Order of St. Francis. In the chronicles of that Order we are told that he had a tender devotion to the Mother of God; and that when he was at the point of death his former life and the rigors of divine justice presented themselves before his mind, and caused him to tremble at the thought of death, and fear for his eternal salvation. Scarcely had these thoughts entered his mind when Mary (who is always active when her servants are in pain), accompanied by many saints, presented herself before the dying man, and encouraged him with words of the greatest tenderness, saying: " My own beloved Adolph, thou art mine, thou hast given thyself to me, and now why dost thou fear death so much?" On hearing these words the servant of Mary was instantly relieved, fear was banished from his soul, and he expired in the midst of the greatest peace and joy.

Let us, then, be of good heart, though we be sinners, and feel certain that Mary will come and assist us at death, and comfort and console us with her presence, provided only that we serve her with love during the remainder of the time that we have to be in this world. Our Queen, one day addressing St. Matilda, promised that she would assist all her clients at death who, during their lives, had faithfully served her. " I, as a most tender mother, will faithfully be present at the death of all who piously serve me, and will console and protect them." O God, what a consolation will it be at that last moment of our lives, when our eternal lot has so soon to be decided, to see the Queen of heaven assisting and consoling us with the assurance of her protection.

Besides the cases already given in which we have seen Mary assisting her dying servants there are innumerable others recorded in different works. This favor was granted to St. Clare; to St. Felix, of the Order of Capuchins; to St. Clare of Montefalco; to St. Teresa; to St. Peter of Alcantara. But, for our common consolation, I will relate the following: Father Crasset tells us, that Mary of Oignies saw the Blessed Virgin at the pillow of a devout widow of Willembroc, who was ill with a violent fever. Mary stood by her side, consoling her, and cooling her with a fan. Of St. John of God, who was tenderly devoted to Mary, it is related that he fully expected that she would visit him on his death-bed; but not seeing her arrive, he was afflicted, and perhaps even complained. But when his last hour had come, the divine Mother appeared, and gently reproving him for his little confidence, addressed him in the following tender words, which may well encourage all servants of Mary: " John, it is not in me to forsake my clients at such a moment." As though she had said: " John, of what wast thou thinking? Didst thou imagine I had abandoned thee? And dost thou not know that I never abandon my clients at the hour of death? If I did not come sooner it was that thy time was not yet come; but now that it is come, behold me here to take thee; let us go to heaven." Shortly afterwards the saint expired, and fled to that blessed kingdom, there to thank his most loving Queen for all eternity.

Prayer.

O my most sweet Mother, how shall I die, poor sinner that I am ? Even now the thought of that important moment when I must expire, and appear before the judgment-seat of God, and the remembrance that I have myself so often written my condemnation by consenting to sin, makes me tremble. I am confounded, and fear much for my eternal salvation. O Mary, in the blood of Jesus, and in thy intercession, is all my hope. Thou art the Queen of heaven, the mistress of the universe; in short, thou art the Mother of God. Thou art great, but thy greatness does not prevent, nay, even it inclines thee to greater compassion towards us in our miseries. Worldly friends when raised to dignity disdain to notice their former friends who may have fallen into distress. Thy noble and loving heart does not act thus, for the greater the miseries it beholds the greater are its efforts to relieve. Thou, when called upon, dost immediately assist; nay, more, thou dost anticipate our prayers by thy favors; thou consolest us in our afflictions; thou dissipatest the storms by which we are tossed about; thou overcomest all enemies; thou, in fine, never losest an occasion to promote our welfare. May that divine hand which has united in thee such majesty and such tenderness, such greatness and so much love, be forever blessed! I thank my Lord for it, and congratulate myself in having so great an advantage; for truly in thy felicity do I place my own, and I consider thy lot as mine. O comfortress of the afflicted, console a poor creature who recommends himself to thee. The remorse of a conscience overburdened with sins fills me with affliction. I am in doubt as to whether I have sufficiently grieved for them. I see that all my actions are sullied and defective; hell awaits my death in order to accuse me; the outraged justice of God demands satisfaction. My Mother, what will become of me? If thou dost not help me, I am lost. What sayest thou, wilt thou assist me? O compassionate Virgin, console me; obtain for me true sorrow for my sins; obtain for me strength to amend, and to be faithful to God during the rest of my life. And finally, when I am in the last agonies of death, O Mary, my hope, abandon me not; then, more than ever, help and encourage me, that I may not despair at the sight of my sins, which the evil one will then place before me. My Lady, forgive my temerity; come thyself to comfort me with thy presence in that last struggle. This favor thou hast granted to many, grant it also to me. If my boldness is great, thy goodness is greater; for it goes in search of the most miserable to console them. On this I rely. For thy eternal glory, let it be said that thou hast snatched a wretched creature from hell, to which he was already condemned, and that thou hast led him to thy kingdom. Oh, yes, sweet Mother, I hope to have the consolation of remaining always at thy feet in heaven, thanking and blessing and loving thee eternally. O Mary, I shall expect thee at my last hour; deprive me not of this consolation. *Fiat, fiat.* Amen, amen.

CHAPTER III.

Spes nostra ! salve.

MARY, OUR HOPE.

I. Mary is the Hope of All.

MODERN heretics cannot endure that we should
salute and call Mary our hope: "Hail, our hope!"
They say that God alone is our hope; and that He
curses those who put their trust in creatures in these
words of the prophet Jeremias: "Cursed be the man
that trusteth in man."* Mary, they exclaim, is a
creature; and how can a creature be our hope? This
is what the heretics say; but in spite of this the holy
Church obliges all ecclesiastics and religious each
day to raise their voices, and in name of all the faithful invoke and call Mary by the sweet name of "our
hope," the hope of all.

The angelical doctor St. Thomas says,† that we
can place our hope in a person in two ways: as a
principal cause, and as a mediate one. Those who
hope for a favor from a king hope it from him as
lord; they hope for it from his minister or favorite as
an intercessor. If the favor is granted, it comes pri-
marily from the king, but it comes through the instrumentality of the favorite; and in this case he who
seeks the favor is right in calling his intercessor his

* Jer. xvii. 5.　　　† 2. 2, q. 25, a. 1, ad 3.

hope. The King of heaven, being infinite goodness, desires in the highest degree to enrich us with His graces; but because confidence is requisite on our part, and in order to increase it in us, He has given us His own Mother to be our Mother and advocate, and to her He has given all power to help us; and therefore He wills that we should repose our hope of salvation and of every blessing in her. Those who place their hopes in creatures alone, independently of God, as sinners do, and in order to obtain the friendship and favor of a man fear not to outrage His divine majesty, are most certainly cursed by God, as the prophet Jeremias says. But those who hope in Mary, as Mother of God, who is able to obtain graces and eternal life for them, are truly blessed and acceptable to the heart of God, Who desires to see that greatest of His creatures honored; for she loved and honored Him in this world more than all men and angels put together. And therefore we justly and reasonably call the Blessed Virgin our hope, trusting, as Cardinal Bellarmine says, "that we shall obtain through her intercession that which we should not obtain by our own unaided prayers." "We pray to her," says the learned Suarez, "in order that the dignity of the intercessor may supply for our own unworthiness; so that," he continues, "to implore the Blessed Virgin in such a spirit is not diffidence in the mercy of God, but fear of our own unworthiness." *

It is, then, not without reason that the holy Church, in the words of Ecclesiasticus, calls Mary " the Mother of holy hope."† She is the Mother who gives birth to holy hope in our hearts; not to the hope of the

* *De Inc.* p. 2, d. 23, s. 3. † Ecclus. xxiv. 24.

vain and transitory goods of this life, but of the immense and eternal goods of heaven.

"Hail, then, O hope of my soul!" exclaims St. Ephrem, addressing this divine Mother; "hail, O certain salvation of Christians; hail, O helper of sinners; hail, fortress of the faithful and salvation of the world!" * Other saints remind us, that after God our only hope is Mary; and therefore they call her, "after God, their only hope." †

St. Ephrem, reflecting on the present order of Providence, by which God wills (as St. Bernard says, and as we shall prove at length) that all who are saved should be saved by the means of Mary, thus addresses her: "O Lady, cease not to watch over us; preserve and guard us under the wings of thy compassion and mercy, for, after God, we have no hope but in thee." ‡ St. Thomas of Villanova repeats the same thing, calling her "our only refuge, help, and asylum." § St. Bernard seems to give the reason for this when he says, "See, O man, the designs of God— designs by which He is able to dispense His mercy more abundantly to us; for, desiring to redeem the whole human race, He has placed the whole price of redemption in the hands of Mary, that she may dispense it at will." ‖

In the Book of Exodus we read that God commanded Moses to make a mercy-seat of the purest gold, because it was thence that He would speak to him. "Thou shalt make also a propitiatory of the purest gold. . . . Thence will I give orders, and will speak to thee." ¶ St. Andrew of Crete says that "the

---

* *De Laud. Dei Gen.*
† *Cant. p. Psalt.*
‡ *De Laud. Dei Gen.*
§ *In Nat. B. V. Conc.* 3.
‖ *De Aquæd.*
¶ Exod. xxv. 17.

whole world embraces Mary as being this propitiatory." And commenting on his words a pious author
exclaims, " Thou, O Mary, art the propitiatory of the
whole world. From thee does our most compassionate Lord speak to our hearts; from thee He speaks
words of pardon and mercy; from thee He bestows His
gifts; from thee all good flows to us." * And therefore, before the Divine Word took flesh in the womb
of Mary, He sent an archangel to ask her consent:
because He willed that the world should receive the
Incarnate Word through her, and that she should be
the source of every good. Hence St. Irenæus remarks, that as Eve was seduced by a fallen angel to
flee from God, so Mary was led to receive God into
her womb, obeying a good angel ; and thus by her
obedience repaired Eve's disobedience, and became
her advocate, and that of the whole human race. " If
Eve disobeyed God, yet Mary was persuaded to obey
God, that the Virgin Mary might become the advocate of the virgin Eve. And as the human race was
bound to death through a virgin, it is saved through a
virgin." † And Blessed Raymond Jordano also says,
" that every good, every help, every grace that men
have received and will receive from God until the
end of time, came, and will come, to them by the intercession and through the hands of Mary." ‡

The devout Blosius, then, might well exclaim, " O
Mary, O thou who art so loving and gracious towards
all who love thee, tell me, who can be so infatuated
and unfortunate as not to love thee ? Thou, in the
midst of their doubts and difficulties, enlightenest the

* *Paciucch. in Sal. Ang. Exc.* 20.
† *Ap. C. à Lap. In Prov.* xxxi. 29,
‡ *Cont. B. M. in. prol.*

minds of all who, in their afflictions, have recourse to thee. Thou encouragest those who fly to thee in time of danger; thou succorest those who call upon thee; thou, after thy divine Son, art the certain salvation of thy faithful servants. Hail, then, O hope of those who are in despair; O succor of those who are abandoned. O Mary, thou art all-powerful; for thy divine Son, to honor thee, complies instantly with all thy desires." *

St. Germanus, recognizing in Mary the source of all our good, and that she delivers us from every evil, thus invokes her: "O my sovereign Lady, thou alone art the one whom God has appointed to be my solace here below; thou art the guide of my pilgrimage, the strength of my weakness, the riches of my poverty, the remedy for the healing of my wounds, the soother of my pains, the end of my captivity, the hope of my salvation! Hear my prayers, have pity on my tears, I conjure thee, O thou who art my queen, my refuge, my love, my help, my hope, and my strength." †

We need not, then, be surprised that St. Antoninus applies the following verse of the Book of Wisdom to Mary: " Now all good things came to me together with her." ‡ For as this Blessed Virgin is the Mother and dispenser of all good things, the whole world, and more particularly each individual who lives in it as a devout client of this great Queen, may say with truth, that with devotion to Mary both he and the world have obtained everything good and perfect. The saint thus expresses his thought: "She is the Mother of all good things, and the world can truly say, that with her (that is, the most blessed Virgin) it has received all good things." § And hence the blessed Abbot of Celles

---

* *Par. an.* p. 2, c. 4. 　　† *Encom. in S. Deip.*
‡ Wis. vii. 11. 　　§ P. 4, l. 15, c. 20, § 12.

expressly declares, "that when we find Mary, we find all." * Whoever finds Mary finds every good thing, obtains all graces and all virtues; for by her powerful intercession she obtains all that is necessary to enrich him with divine grace. In the Book of Proverbs Mary herself tells us that she possesses all the riches of God, that is to say, His mercies, that she may dispense them in favor of her lovers: "With me are riches . . . and glorious riches . . . that I may enrich them that love me." † And therefore St. Bonaventure says, "that we ought all to keep our eyes constantly fixed on Mary's hands, that through them we may receive the graces that we desire." ‡

Oh, how many who were once proud have become humble by devotion to Mary! how many who were passionate have become meek ! how many in the midst of darkness have found light ! how many who were in despair have found confidence ! how many who were lost have found salvation by the same powerful means! And this she clearly foretold in the house of Elizabeth, in her own sublime canticle: "Behold, from henceforth all generations shall call me blessed." And St. Bernard, interpreting her words, says: "All generations call thee blessed, because thou hast given life and glory to all nations,§ for in thee sinners find pardon, and the just perseverance in the grace of God." ‖

Hence the devout Lanspergius makes Our Lord thus address the world: " Men, poor children of Adam, who live surrounded by so many enemies, and in the midst of so many trials, endeavor to honor My Mother and yours in a special manner: for I have given Mary to the world that she may be your model,

---

* *De Cont. de V. M. in Prol.*   † Prov. viii. 18.
‡ *Spec. B. V. lect.* 3.   § *In Pentec.* s. 2.   ‖ *In Pent.* s. 2.

and that from her you may learn to lead good lives; and also that she may be a refuge to which you can fly in all your afflictions and trials. I have rendered this, my daughter, such that no one need fear or have the least repugnance to have recourse to her; and for this purpose I have created her of so benign and compassionate a disposition that she knows not how to despise any one who takes refuge with her, nor can she deny her favor to any one who seeks it. The mantle of her mercy is open to all, and she allows no one to leave her feet without consoling him." * May the immense goodness of our God be ever praised and blessed for having given us so great, so tender, so loving a Mother and advocate.

O God, how tender are the sentiments of confidence expressed by the enamoured St. Bonaventure towards Jesus our most loving Redeemer, and Mary our most loving advocate ! He says, " Whatever God foresees to be my lot, I know that He cannot refuse Himself to any one who loves Him and seeks for Him with his whole heart. I will embrace Him with my love; and if He does not bless me, I will still cling to Him so closely that He will be unable to go without me. If I can do nothing else, at least I will hide myself in His wounds, and taking up my dwelling there, it will be in Himself alone that He will find me." And the saint concludes, " If my Redeemer rejects me on account of my sins, and drives me from His sacred feet, I will cast myself at those of His beloved Mother Mary, and there I will remain prostrate until she has obtained my forgiveness; for this Mother of mercy knows not, and has never known, how to do otherwise than compassionate

* *Alloq.* l. 1, p. 4, *can.* 12.

the miserable, and comply with the desires of the most
destitute who fly to her for succor; and therefore," he
says, " if not by duty, at least by compassion, she will
engage her Son to pardon me." *

" Look down upon us, then," let us exclaim, in the
words of Euthymius, " look down upon us, O most
compassionate Mother; cast thine eyes of mercy on
us, for we are thy servants, and in thee we have placed
all our confidence." †

Prayer.

O Mother of holy love, our life, our refuge, and our
hope, thou well knowest that thy Son Jesus Christ, not
content with being Himself our perpetual advocate with
the Eternal Father, has willed that thou also shouldst
interest thyself with Him, in order to obtain the divine
mercies for us. He has decreed that thy prayers should
aid our salvation, and has made them so efficacious that
they obtain all that they ask. To thee therefore, who art
the hope of the miserable, do I, a wretched sinner, turn
my eyes. I trust, O Lady, that in the first place through
the merits of Jesus Christ, and then through thy intercession, I shall be saved. Of this I am certain ; and my
confidence in thee is such that if my eternal salvation
were in my own hands I should place it in thine, for I
rely more on thy mercy and protection than on all my
own works. My Mother and my hope, abandon me not,
though I deserve that thou shouldst do so. See my
miseries, and, being moved thereby with compassion,
help and save me. I own that I have too often closed
my heart, by my sins, against the lights and helps that
thou hast procured for me from the Lord. But thy compassion for the miserable, and thy power with God, far

* *Stim. div. am.* p. 3, c. 13.   † *Ap. Sur.* 31 *Aug.*

surpass the number and malice of my sins. It is well
known to all, both in heaven and on earth, that whoso-
ever is protected by thee is certainly saved. All may
forget me, provided only that thou dost remember me,
O Mother of an omnipotent God. Tell Him that I am
thy servant; say only that thou defendest me, and I shall
be saved. O Mary, I trust in thee; in this hope I live;
in it I desire and hope to die, repeating always, "Jesus
is my only hope, and after Jesus the most blessed Virgin
Mary."

II. Mary is the Hope of Sinners.

In the first chapter of the Book of Genesis we read
that " God made two great lights; a greater light to
rule the day, and a lesser light to rule the night. " *
Cardinal Hugo says that " Christ is the greater light
to rule the just, and Mary the lesser to rule sinners; "
meaning that the sun is a figure of Jesus Christ, Whose
light is enjoyed by the just who live in the clear day
of divine grace; and that the moon is a figure of
Mary, by whose means those who are in the night of
sin are enlightened. Since Mary is this auspicious
luminary, and is so for the benefit of poor sinners,
should any one have been so unfortunate as to fall
into the night of sin, what is he to do? Innocent
III. replies, " Whoever is in the night of sin, let him
cast his eyes on the moon, let him implore Mary." †
Since he has lost the light of the sun of justice by
losing the grace of God, let him turn to the moon,
and beseech Mary; and she will certainly give him
light to see the misery of his state, and strength to
leave it without delay. St. Methodius says " that by

* Gen. i. 16.   † *In Assumpt.* s. 2.

the prayers of Mary almost innumerable sinners are converted." *

One of the titles which is the most encouraging to poor sinners, and under which the Church teaches us to invoke Mary in the Litany of Loretto, is that of "refuge of sinners." In Judea in ancient times there were cities of refuge, in which criminals who fled there for protection were exempt from the punishments which they had deserved. Nowadays these cities are not so numerous; there is but one, and that is Mary, of whom the psalmist says, " Glorious things are said of thee, O city of God." † But this city differs from the ancient ones in this respect—that in the latter all kinds of criminals did not find refuge, nor was the protection extended to every class of crime; but under the mantle of Mary all sinners, without exception, find refuge for every sin that they may have committed, provided only that they go there to seek for this protection. " I am the city of refuge," says St. John Damascene, in the name of our Queen, " to all who fly to me." ‡ And it is sufficient to have recourse to her, for whoever has the good fortune to enter this city need not speak to be saved. " Assemble yourselves, and let us enter into the fenced city, and let us be silent there," § to speak in the words of the prophet Jeremias. This city, says Blessed Albert the Great, is the most holy Virgin fenced in with grace and glory. " And let us be silent there," that is, continues an interpreter, " because we dare not invoke the Lord, Whom we have offended; she will invoke and ask." ‖ For if we do not presume to ask

---

* *Paciucch. in Ps.* lxxxvi. *exc.* 17.   † Ps. lxxxvi. 3.
‡ *In Dorm. B. V. or.* 2.   § Jer. viii. 14.
‖ *Bib. Mar. Jer.* n. 3.

Our Lord to forgive us, it will suffice to enter this
city and be silent, for Mary will speak and ask all that
we require.   And for this reason a devout author exhorts all sinners to take refuge under the mantle of
Mary, exclaiming, " Fly, O Adam and Eve, and all
you their children who have outraged God—fly, and
take refuge in the bosom of this good Mother; know
you not that she is our only city of refuge ? " * " the
only hope of sinners," † as she is also called in a sermon by an ancient writer, found in the works of St.
Augustine.

St. Ephrem, addressing the Blessed Virgin, says,
" Thou art the only advocate of sinners, and of all
who are unprotected."   And then he salutes her in
the following words: " Hail, refuge and hospital of
sinners ! " ‡—true refuge, in which alone they can
hope for reception and liberty.   And an author remarks that this was the meaning of David when he
said, " For He hath hidden me in His tabernacle." §
And truly what can this tabernacle of God be, unless
it is Mary ? who is called by St. Germanus, " A tabernacle made by God, in which He alone entered to ac-
complish the great work of the redemption of man." ‖

St. Basil of Seleucia remarks, " that if God granted
to some who were only His servants such power that
not only their touch but even their shadows healed
the sick, who were placed for this purpose in the public streets, how much greater power must we suppose
that He has granted to her who was not only His
handmaid but His Mother ? "   We may indeed say
that Our Lord has given us Mary as a public infirm-

* *B. Fernandez in Gen.* c. 3, s. 22.
† *Serm.* 194, *E. B. app.*   ‡ *De Laud. Dei gen.*
§ Ps. xxvi. 5.   ‖ *In Nat. S. M. or.* 2.

ary, in which all who are sick, poor, and destitute can
be received. But now I ask, in hospitals erected expressly for the poor, who have the greatest claim to
admission ? Certainly the most infirm, and those who
are in the greatest need.

And for this reason should any one find himself devoid of merit and overwhelmed with spiritual infirmi-
ties, that is to say, sin, he can thus address Mary: O
Lady, thou art the refuge of the sick poor; reject me
not; for as I am the poorest and the most infirm of
all, I have the greatest right to be welcomed by thee.

Let us then cry out with St. Thomas of Villanova,
" O Mary, we poor sinners know no other refuge than
thee, for thou art our only hope, and on thee we rely
for our salvation." * Thou art our only advocate
with Jesus Christ; to thee we all turn ourselves.

In the revelations of St. Bridget Mary is called the
" star preceding the sun," † giving us thereby to understand that when devotion towards the divine
Mother begins to manifest itself in a soul that is in a
state of sin it is a certain mark that before long God
will enrich it with His grace. The glorious St. Bonaventure, in order to revive the confidence of sinners
in the protection of Mary, places before them the
picture of a tempestuous sea, into which sinners have
already fallen from the ship of divine grace; they are
already dashed about on every side by remorse of
conscience and by fear of the judgments of God ;
they are without light or guide, and are on the point
of losing the last breath of hope and falling into despair; then it is that Our Lord, pointing out Mary to
them, who is commonly called the " star of the sea,"

* *De Nat. V. M. conc.* 3.   † *Rev. Extr.* c. 50.

raises His voice and says, " O poor lost sinners, despair not; raise up your eyes, and cast them on this
beautiful star; breathe again with confidence, for it
will save you from this tempest, and will guide you
into the port of salvation."* St. Bernard says the
same thing: " If thou wouldst not be lost in the tempest, cast thine eyes on the star, and invoke Mary." †

The devout Blosius declares that " she is the only
refuge of those who have offended God, the asylum
of all who are oppressed by temptation, calamity, or
persecution. This Mother is all mercy, benignity,
and sweetness, not only to the just, but also to despairing sinners; so that no sooner does she perceive
them coming to her, and seeking her health from their
hearts, than she aids them, welcomes them, and obtains their pardon from her Son. She knows not how
to despise any one, however unworthy he may be of
mercy, and therefore denies her protection to none; she
consoles all, and is no sooner called upon than she
helps whoever it may be that invokes her. She by her
sweetness often awakens and draws sinners to her devotion who are the most at enmity with God and the
most deeply plunged in the lethargy of sin; and then,
by the same means, she excites them effectually, and
prepares them for grace, and thus renders them fit for
the kingdom of heaven. God has created this His
beloved daughter of so compassionate and sweet a
disposition that no one can fear to have recourse to
her." The pious author concludes in these words:
" It is impossible for any one to perish who atten-
tively, and with humility, cultivates devotion towards
this divine Mother." ‡

* *Psal. B. V. ps.* 18.   † *De Laud. V. M. hom.* 2.
‡ *Par. an. fid.* p. 1, c. 18.

In Ecclesiasticus Mary is called a plane-tree: "As a plane-tree I was exalted." * And she is so called that sinners may understand that as the plane-tree gives shelter to travellers from the heat of the sun, so does Mary invite them to take shelter under her protection from the wrath of God, justly enkindled against them. St. Bonaventure remarks that the prophet Isaias complained of the times in which he lived, saying, "Behold Thou art angry, and we have sinned; . . . there is none . . . that riseth up and taketh hold of Thee." † And then he makes the following commentary: "It is true, O Lord, that at the time there was none to raise up sinners, and withhold Thy wrath, for Mary was not yet born;" "before Mary," to quote the saint's own words, "there was no one who could thus dare to restrain the arm of God." But now, if God is angry with a sinner, and Mary takes him under her protection, she withholds the avenging arm of her Son, and saves him. "And so," continues the same saint, "no one can be found more fit for this office than Mary, who seizes the sword of divine justice with her own hands to prevent it from falling upon and punishing the sinner." ‡ Upon the same subject Richard of St. Laurence says that "God, before the birth of Mary, complained by the mouth of the prophet Ezechiel that there was no one to rise up and withhold Him from chastising sinners, but that He could find no one, for this office was reserved for our blessed Lady, who withholds His arm until He is pacified." §

Basil of Seleucia encourages sinners, saying, "O sinner, be not discouraged, but have recourse to Mary in all thy necessities; call her to thine assistance, for

---

* Ecclus. xxiv. 19.   † Is. lxiv. 5.

‡ *Spec. B. V. lect.* 7, 14.   § *De Laud. B. M.* l. 2, p. 5.

thou wilt always find her ready to help thee; for such
is the divine will that she should help all in every kind
of necessity."* This Mother of mercy has so great
a desire to save the most abandoned sinners that she
herself goes in search of them, in order to help
them; and if they have recourse to her, she knows
how to find the means to render them acceptable to
God.   The patriarch Isaac, desiring to eat of some
wild animal, promised his blessing to his son Esau on
his procuring this food for him; but Rebecca, who was
anxious that her other son Jacob should receive the
blessing, called him and said, "Go thy way to the
flock, bring me two kids of the best, that I may make
of them meat for thy father, such as he gladly eat-
eth."†   St. Antoninus says, ‡ "that Rebecca was a
figure of Mary, who commands the angels to bring her
sinners (meant by kids), that she may adorn them in
such a way (by obtaining for them sorrow and purpose of amendment) as to render them dear and acceptable to the Lord."   And here we may well apply
to our blessed Lady the words of the Abbot Franco:
"O truly sagacious woman, who so well knew how to
dress these kids that not only are they equal to, but
often superior in flavor to, real venison."§

The Blessed Virgin herself revealed to St. Bridget
"that there is no sinner in the world, however much
he may be at enmity with God, who does not return
to Him and recover His grace, if he has recourse to her
and asks her assistance." ‖   The same St. Bridget one
day heard Jesus Christ address His Mother, and say
that "she would be ready to obtain the grace of God

* *Paciucch. in Salve R. exc.* 7.
† Gen. xxvii. 9.   ‡ P. 4, t. 15, c. 2, § 2.
§ *De Grat. D.* l. 3.   ‖ Rev. l. 6, c. 10.

for Lucifer himself, if only he humbled himself so far
as to seek her aid."* That proud spirit will never
himself so far as to implore the protection of Mary;
but if such a thing were possible, Mary would be sufficiently compassionate, and her prayers would have
sufficient power, to obtain both forgiveness and salvation for him from God. But that which cannot be
verified with regard to the devil is verified in the case
of sinners who have recourse to this compassionate
Mother.

Noe's ark was a true figure of Mary; for as in it all
kinds of beasts were saved, so under the mantle of
Mary all sinners, who by their vices and sensuality are
already like beasts, find refuge; but with this differ-
ence, as a pious author remarks, that " while the brutes
that entered the ark remained brutes, the wolf remaining a wolf, and a tiger a tiger—under the mantle
of Mary, on the other hand, the wolf becomes a lamb,
and the tiger a dove."† One day St. Gertrude saw
Mary with her mantle open, and under it there were
many wild beasts of different kinds—leopards, lions,
and bears; and she saw that not only our blessed
Lady did not drive them away, but that she welcomed
and caressed them with her benign hand. The saint
understood that these wild beasts were miserable sinners, who are welcomed by Mary with sweetness and
love the moment they have recourse to her.‡

It was, then, not without reason that St. Bernard
addressed the Blessed Virgin, saying, " Thou, O Lady,
dost not reject any sinner who approaches thee, however loathsome and repugnant he may be. If he asks
thy assistance, thou dost not disdain to extend thy

* *Rev. extr.* c. 50.
† *Paciucch. in Sal. Ang. exc.* 4.   ‡ *Insin.* l. 4, c. 50.

compassionate hand to him, to extricate him from the gulf of despair." *   May our God be eternally blessed and thanked, O most amiable Mary, for having created thee so sweet and benign, even towards the most miserable sinners!   Truly unfortunate is he who loves thee not, and who, having it in his power to obtain thy assistance, has no confidence in thee.   He who has not recourse to Mary is lost; but who was ever lost that had recourse to the most blessed Virgin ?

It is related in the Sacred Scriptures that Booz allowed Ruth "to gather the ears of corn after the reapers." †   St. Bonaventure says, " that as Ruth found favor with Booz, so has Mary found favor with Our Lord, and is also allowed to gather the ears of corn after the reapers.   The reapers followed by Mary are all evangelical laborers, missionaries, preachers, and confessors, who are constantly reaping souls for God.   But there are some hardened and rebellious souls which are abandoned even by these.   To Mary alone it is granted to save them by her powerful intercession." ‡   Truly unfortunate are they if they do not allow themselves to be gathered, even by this sweet Lady.   They will indeed be most certainly lost and accursed.   But, on the other hand, blessed is he who has recourse to this good Mother.   "There is not in the world," says the devout Blosius, " any sinner, however revolting and wicked, who is despised or rejected by Mary; she can, she wills, and she knows how to reconcile him to her most beloved Son, if only he will seek her assistance." §

With reason then, O my most sweet Queen, did St. John Damascene salute and call thee the " hope of

* *Depr. ad B. V.*   † Ruth ii. 3.
‡ *Spec. B. V. M. lect.* 5.   § *Sac. an. fid.* p. 3, c. 5.

those who are in despair." With reason did St. Laurence Justinian call thee " the hope of malefactors," and another ancient writer " the only hope of sinners." St. Ephrem calls her " the safe harbor of all sailing on the sea of the world." This last-named saint also calls her " the consolation of those who are to be condemned." With reason, finally, does St. Bernard exhort even the desperate not to despair; and, full of joy and tenderness towards his most dear Mother, he lovingly exclaims: "And who, O Lady, can be without confidence in thee, since thou assistest even those who are in despair? And I doubt not that whenever we have recourse to thee we shall obtain all that we desire. Let him, then, who is without hope, hope in thee."* St. Antoninus relates † that there was a sinner who was at enmity with God, and who had a vision in which he found himself before the dread tribunal; the devil accused him, and Mary defended him. The enemy produced the catalogue of his sins; it was thrown into the scales of divine justice, and weighed far more than all his good works. But then his great advocate, extending her sweet hand, placed it on the balance, and so caused it to turn in favor of her client; giving him thereby to understand that she would obtain his pardon if he changed his life; and this he did after the vision, and was entirely converted.

Prayer.

O most pure Virgin Mary, I venerate thy most holy heart, which was the delight and resting place of God, thy heart overflowing with humility, purity, and divine love. I, an unhappy sinner, approach thee with a heart

---

* *Med. in Salv. R.*   † P. 4, t. 15, c. 5, § 1.

all loathsome and wounded. O compassionate Mother, disdain me not on this account ; let such a sight rather move thee to greater tenderness, and excite thee to help me.   Do not stay to seek virtues or merit in me before assisting me.   I am lost, and the only thing I merit is hell.   See only my confidence in thee and the purpose I have to amend.   Consider all that Jesus has done and suffered for me, and then abandon me if thou canst.   I offer thee all the pains of His life ; the cold that He endured in the stable ; His journey into Egypt ; the blood which He shed ; the poverty, sweats, sorrows, and death that He endured for me ; and this in thy presence.   For the love of Jesus, take charge of my salvation.   Ah, my Mother, I will not and cannot fear that thou wilt reject me, now that I have recourse to thee and ask thy help. Did I fear this, I should be offering an outrage to thy mercy, which goes in quest of the wretched, in order to help them.   O Lady, deny not thy compassion to one to whom Jesus has not denied His blood.   But the merits of this blood will not be applied to me unless thou recommendest me to God.   Through thee do I hope for salvation.   I ask not for riches, honors, or earthly goods. I seek only the grace of God, love towards thy Son, the accomplishment of His will, and His heavenly kingdom, that I may love Him eternally.   Is it possible that thou wilt not hear me ?   No ; for already thou hast granted my prayer, as I hope ; already thou prayest for me ; already thou obtainest me the graces that I ask ; already thou takest me under thy protection.   My Mother, abandon me not.   Never, never cease to pray for me, until thou seest me safe in heaven at thy feet, blessing and thanking thee forever.   Amen.

CHAPTER IV.

Ad te clamamus, exsules filii Evæ.

TO THEE DO WE CRY, POOR BANISHED CHILDREN OF EVE.

MARY, OUR HELP.

I. The Promptitude of Mary in assisting those who invoke her.

TRULY unfortunate are we poor children of Eve; for, guilty before God of her fault, and condemned to the same penalty, we have to wander about in this valley of tears as exiles from our country, and to weep over our many afflictions of body and soul. But blessed is he who, in the midst of these sorrows, often turns to the comfortress of the world, to the refuge of the unfortunate, to the great Mother of God, and devoutly calls upon her and invokes her! " Blessed is the man that heareth me, and that watcheth daily at my gates." * Blessed, says Mary, is he who listens to my counsels, and watches continually at the gate of my mercy, and invokes my intercession and aid.

The holy Church carefully teaches us her children with what attention and confidence we should unceasingly have recourse to this loving protectress; and for this purpose commands a worship peculiar to Mary. And not only this, but she has instituted so many

* Prov. viii. 34.

festivals that are celebrated through the year in honor
of this great Queen; she devotes one day in the week,
in an especial manner, to her honor; in the divine
office all ecclesiastics and religious are daily obliged
to invoke her in the name of all Christians; and,
finally, she desires that all the faithful should salute
this most holy Mother of God three times a day, at
the sound of the Angelus-bell. And that we may
understand the confidence that the holy Church has in
Mary, we need only remember that in all public calam-
ities she invariably invites all to have recourse to the
protection of this divine Mother, by novenas, prayers,
processions, by visiting the churches dedicated in her
honor, and her images. And this is what Mary desires. She wishes us always to seek her and invoke
her aid; not as if she were begging of us these honors
and marks of veneration, for they are in no way pro-
portioned to her merit; but she desires them, that
by such means our confidence and devotion may be
increased, and that so she may be able to give us
greater succor and comfort. "She seeks for those,"
says St. Bonaventure, "who approach her devoutly
and with reverence, for such she loves, nourishes, and
adopts as her children." *

This last-named saint remarks, that Ruth, whose
name signifies "seeing and hastening," was a figure of
Mary; "for Mary, seeing our miseries, hastens in her
mercy to succor us." † Novarino adds, that "Mary,
in the greatness of her desire to help us, cannot
admit of· delay, for she is in no way an avaricious
guardian of the graces she has at her disposal as
Mother of mercy, and cannot do otherwise than im-

* *Stim. Am.* p. 3, c. 16.   † *Spec. B. M. V. lect.* v.

mediately shower down the treasures of her liberality
of her servants." *

Oh, how prompt is this good Mother to help those
who call upon her ! " Thy two breasts," says the
sacred Canticle, " are like two roes that are twins." †
Richard of St. Laurence explains this verse, and says,
that as roes are swift in their course, so are the breasts
of Mary prompt to bestow the milk of mercy on all
who ask it. " By the light pressure of a devout salutation and prayer they distil large drops." ‡   The
same author assures us that the compassion of Mary
is poured out on every one who asks it, even should
it be sought for by no other prayer than a simple
" Hail Mary."   Wherefore Novarino declares that the
Blessed Virgin not only runs but flies to assist him
who invokes her. " She," says this author, " in the
exercise of her mercy, knows not how to act differ-
ently from God; for, as He flies at once to the assistance of those who beg His aid, faithful to His promise, ' Ask, and you shall receive,' § so Mary, whenever
she is invoked, is at once ready to assist him who
prays to her.   God has wings when He assists His
own, and immediately flies to them; Mary also takes
wing when she is about to fly to our aid." ‖   And
hence we see who the woman was, spoken of in the
following verse of the Apocalypse, to whom two great
eagle's wings were given, that she might fly to the
desert.   " And there were given to the woman two
wings of a great eagle, that she might fly into the
desert." ¶   Ribeira explains these wings to mean the
love with which Mary always flew to God.   " She has

* *Umbr. Virg. exc.* 73.   † Cant. iv. 5. ·
‡ *De Laud. B. M.* l. 1, c. 8.   § John xvi. 24.
‖ *Umbra Virg. exc.* 73.   ¶ Apoc. xii. 14.

the wings of an eagle, for she flies with the love of
God." But the Blessed Amadeus, more to our purpose, remarks that these wings of an eagle signify
" the velocity, exceeding that of the seraphim, with
which Mary always flies to the succor of her children." *

This will explain a passage in the Gospel of St.
Luke, in which we are told that when Mary went to
visit and shower graces on St. Elizabeth and her whole
family, she was not slow, but went with speed.   The
Gospel says, " And Mary, rising up, went into the hill
country with haste." † And this is not said of her return.   For a similar reason, we are told in the sacred
Canticles that the hands of Mary are used to the lathe:
" Her hands are skilful at the wheel," ‡ meaning, says
Richard of St. Laurence, " that as the art of turning is
the easiest and most expeditious mode of working, so
also is Mary the most willing and prompt of all the saints
to assist her clients." §   And truly " she has the most
ardent desire to console all, and is no sooner invoked
than she accepts the prayers, and helps." ‖   St. Bonaventure, then, was right in calling Mary the " salvation
of all who call upon her," ¶ meaning, that it suffices to
invoke this divine Mother in order to be saved; for, according to Richard of St. Laurence, she is always
ready to help those who seek her aid.   " Thou wilt
always find her ready to help thee." **   And Bernardine de Bustis adds, " that this great Lady is more
desirous to grant us graces than we are desirous to
receive them." ††

* *De Laud. B. V. hom.* 8.   † Luke i. 39.
‡ Cant. v. 14.   § *De Laud. B. M.* l. 5.
‖ *Par. an. fid.* p. 1, c. 18.   ¶ *Cant. p. Psalt.*
** *De Laud. B. M.* l. 2, p. 1.   †† *Marial.* p. 2, s. 5.

Nor should the multitude of our sins diminish **our** confidence that Mary will grant our petitions when we cast ourselves at her feet. She is the Mother of mercy; but mercy would not be needed did none exist who require it. On this subject Richard of St. Laurence remarks, " that as a good Mother does not shrink from applying a remedy to her child infected with ulcers, however nauseous and revolting they may be, so also is our good Mother unable to abandon us when we have recourse to her, that she may heal the wounds caused by our sins, however loathsome they may have rendered us." * This is exactly what Mary gave St. Gertrude to understand when she showed herself to her with her mantle spread out to receive all who have recourse to her. At the same time the saint was told that "angels constantly guard the clients of this Blessed Virgin from the assaults of hell."

This good Mother's compassion is so great, and the love she bears us is such, that she does not even wait for our prayers in order to assist us; but, as it is expressed in the Book of Wisdom, " she preventeth them that covet her, so that she first showeth herself unto them." † St. Anselm applies these words to Mary, and says that she is beforehand with those who desire her protection. By this we are to understand that she obtains us many favors from God before we have recourse to her. For this reason Richard of St. Victor remarks, that she is called the moon, "fair as the moon," ‡ meaning, not only that she is swift as the moon in its course, by flying to the aid of those who invoke her, but that she is still more so, for her love for us is so tender that in our wants she anticipates our

---

* *De Laud. B. M.* l. 4.   † Wis. vi. 14.   ‡ Cant. vi. 9.

prayers, and her mercy is more prompt to help us than we are to ask her aid. "And this arises," adds the same Richard, "from the fact that the heart of Mary is so filled with compassion for poor sinners that she no sooner sees our miseries than she pours her tender mercies upon us. Nor is it possible for this benign Queen to behold the want of any soul without immediately assisting it." *

Mary, even when living in this world, showed at the marriage-feast of Cana the great compassion that she would afterwards exercise towards us in our necessities, and which now, as it were, forces her to have pity on us, and assist us, even before we ask her to do so. In the second chapter of St. Luke we read that at this feast the compassionate Mother saw the embarrassment in which the bride and bridegroom were, and that they were quite ashamed on seeing the wine fail; and therefore, without being asked, and listening only to the dictates of her compassionate heart, which could never behold the afflictions of others without feeling for them, she begged her Son to console them simply by laying their distress before Him: "They have no wine." † No sooner had she done so than Our Lord, in order to satisfy all present, and still more to console the compassionate heart of His Mother, who had asked the favor, worked the well-known miracle by which He changed the water, brought to Him in jars, into wine. From this Novarinus argues that "if Mary, unasked, is thus prompt to succor the needy, how much more so will she be to succor those who invoke her and ask for her help?" ‡

Should there be any one who doubts as to whether

* *In Cant.* c. 23. † John ii. 3,
‡ *Umbra Virg. exc. 7?*

Mary will aid him if he has recourse to her, Innocent III. thus reproves him : " Who is there that ever, when in the night of sin, had recourse to this sweet Lady without being relieved ? " *

" Who ever," exclaims the Blessed Eutychian,† " faithfully implored thy all-powerful aid and was abandoned by thee ? " Indeed, no one : for thou canst relieve the most wretched and save the most abandoned. Such a case certainly never did and never will occur.

" I am satisfied," says St. Bernard, " that whoever has had recourse to thee, O Blessed Virgin, in his wants, and can remember that he did so in vain, should no more speak of or praise thy mercy." ‡

" Sooner," says the devout Blosius, " would heaven and earth be destroyed than would Mary fail to assist any one who asks for her help, provided he does so with a good intention and with confidence in her." §

St. Anselm, to increase our confidence, adds, that " when we have recourse to this divine Mother, not only we may be sure of her protection, but that often we shall be heard more quickly, and be thus preserved, if we have recourse to Mary and call on her holy name, than we should be if we called on the name of Jesus our Saviour ; " and the reason he gives for it is, " that to Jesus, as a judge, it belongs also to punish ; but mercy alone belongs to the Blessed Virgin as a patroness." ‖   Meaning, that we more easily find sal-vation by having recourse to the Mother than by going to the Son—not as if Mary was more powerful than her Son to save us, for we know that Jesus Christ

* *De Assumpt.* s. 2.   † *Vit. S. Theoph. ap. Sur.* 4 *Febr.*
‡ *De Assumpt.* s. 4.   § *Consol. pusil.* c. 35.
‖ *De Excell. V.* c. 6.

is our only Saviour, and that He alone by His merits has obtained and obtains salvation for us ; but it is for this reason: that when we have recourse to Jesus, we consider Him at the same time as our judge, to Whom it belongs also to chastise ungrateful souls, and therefore the confidence necessary to be heard may fail us; but when we go to Mary, who has no other office than to compassionate us as Mother of mercy, and to defend us as our advocate, our confidence is more easily established, and is often greater. "We often obtain more promptly what we ask by calling on the name of Mary than by invoking that of Jesus. Her Son is lord and judge of all, and discerns the merits of each one; and therefore if He does not immediately grant the prayers of all, He is just. When, however, the Mother's name is invoked, though the merits of the suppliant are not such as to deserve that his prayer should be granted, those of the Mother supply that he may receive."

"Many things," says Nicephorus, " are asked from God, and are not granted : they are asked from Mary, and are obtained." And how is this? It is "because God has thus decreed to honor His Mother." St. Bridget heard Our Lord make a most sweet and consoling promise; for in the fiftieth chapter of the first book of her revelations we read that Jesus addressed His Mother in the following words : "Thou shalt present Me with no petition that shall be refused. My Mother, ask what thou wilt, for never will I refuse thee anything ; and know," He added, "that I promise graciously to hear all those who ask any favor of Me in thy name, though they may be sinners, if only they have the will to amend their lives." * The same

* Rev. l. i, c. 50.

thing was revealed to St. Gertrude, when she heard
our divine Redeemer assure His Mother that in His
omnipotence He granted her power to show mercy to
sinners who invoke her in whatever manner she might
please.

Let all, then, say, with full confidence in the words
of that beautiful prayer addressed to the Mother of
mercy, and commonly attributed to St. Bernard, "Remember, O most pious Virgin Mary, that it never was
heard of in any age that any one having recourse to
thy protection was abandoned." Therefore forgive
me, O Mary, if I say that I will not be the first unfortunate creature who has ever had recourse to thee
and was abandoned.

Prayer.

O Mother of God, Queen of angels and hope of men,
give ear to one who calls upon thee and has recourse to
thy protection. Behold me this day prostrate at thy feet;
I, a miserable slave of hell, devote myself entirely to thee.
I desire to be forever thy servant. I offer myself to serve
and honor thee to the utmost of my power during the
whole of my life. I know that the service of one so vile
and miserable can be no honor to thee, since I have so
grievously offended Jesus, thy Son and my Redeemer.
But if thou wilt accept one so unworthy for thy servant,
and by thy intercession change me, and thus make me
worthy, this very mercy will give thee that honor which
so miserable a wretch as I can never give thee. Receive
me, then, and reject me not, O my Mother. The Eternal
Word came from heaven on earth to seek for lost sheep,
and to save them He became thy Son. And when one of
them goes to thee to find Jesus, wilt thou despise it? The
price of my salvation is already paid; my Saviour has already shed His blood, which suffices to save an infinity of
worlds. This blood has only to be applied even to such
a one as I am. And that is thy office, O Blessed Virgin;

to thee does it belong, as I am told by St. Bernard, to dispense the merits of this blood to whom thou pleasest. To thee does it belong, says St. Bonaventure, to save whomsoever thou willest, "whomsoever thou willest will be saved." Oh, then, help me, my Queen; my Queen, save me. To thee do I this day consecrate my whole soul; do thou save it. O salvation of those who invoke thee, I conclude in the words of the same saint, " O salvation of those who call upon thee, do thou save me."

II. The Greatness of the Power of Mary to defend those who invoke her when tempted by the Devil.

Not only is the most blessed Virgin Queen of heaven and of all saints, but she is also Queen of hell and of all evil spirits; for she overcame them valiantly by her virtues. From the very beginning God foretold the victory and empire that our Queen would one day obtain over the serpent, when He announced that a woman should come into the world to conquer him: " I will put enmities between thee and the woman— she shall crush thy head."*

Who could this woman, his enemy, be but Mary, who by her fair humility and holy life always conquered him and beat down his strength? The Mother of Our Lord Jesus Christ was promised in the person of that woman,† as it is remarked by St. Cyprian,‡ and after him another ancient writer; and therefore God did not say, " I place," but, " I will place," lest He might seem to refer to Eve : meaning that God said, " I will place enmities between thee and the woman," to signify that the serpent's opponent was not to be Eve, who was then living, but would be another woman descend-

---

* Gen. iii. 15.

† *De Viro perf. inter op. S. Hier.*   ‡ *Test.* l. 2, c. 9.

ing from her, and who, as St. Vincent Ferrer observes, "would bring our first parents far greater advantages than those which they had lost by their sin." * Mary, then, was this great and valiant woman, who conquered the devil and crushed his head by bringing down his pride, as it was foretold by God Himself: "She shall crush thy head." Some doubt as to whether these words refer to Mary, or whether they do not rather refer to Jesus Christ; for the Septuagint renders them, "He shall crush thy head." But in the Vulgate, which alone was approved of by the sacred Council of Trent, we find *she*, and not *he ;* and thus it was understood by St. Ambrose, St. Jerome, St. Augustine, and a great many others. However, be it as it may, it is certain that either the Son by means of the Mother, or the Mother by means of the Son, has overcome Lucifer; so that, as St. Bernard remarks, this proud spirit, in spite of himself, was beaten down and trampled under foot by this most blessed Virgin; so that, as a slave conquered in war, he is forced always to obey the commands of this Queen. "Beaten down and trampled under the feet of Mary, he endured a wretched slavery."† St. Bruno says "that Eve was the cause of death," by allowing herself to be overcome by the serpent, "but that Mary," by conquering the devil, "restored life to us." ‡ And she bound him in such a way that this enemy cannot stir so as to do the least injury to any of her clients.

Beautiful is the explanation given by Richard of St. Laurence of the following words of the Book of Proverbs : "The heart of her husband trusteth in her,

---

* *Serm. de Concep. B. V. M.*
† *In Sign. Magn.*   ‡ *De B. V.* s. 2.

and he shall have no need of spoils." * He says, applying them to Jesus and Mary: "the heart of her spouse, that is, Christ, trusteth in her, and He shall have no need of spoils; for she endows Him with all those whom by her prayers, merits, and example she snatches from the devil." † "God has entrusted the heart of Jesus to the hands of Mary, that she may insure it the love of men," says Cornelius à Lapide; and thus He will not need spoils; that is, He will be abundantly supplied with souls; for she enriches Him with those whom she has snatched from hell, and saved from the devil by her powerful assistance.

It is well known that the palm is a sign of victory; and therefore our Queen is placed on a high throne, in sight of all the powers, as a palm, for a sign of the certain victory that all may promise themselves who place themselves under her protection. "I was exalted like a palm-tree in Cades," ‡ says Ecclesiasticus: "that is, to defend," adds Blessed Albert the Great.§ "My children," Mary seems to say, "when the enemy assails you, fly to me; cast your eyes on me, and be of good heart; for as I am your defender, victory is assured to you." So that recourse to Mary is a most secure means to conquer all the assaults of hell; for she, says St. Bernardine of Siena, is even the Queen of hell and sovereign mistress of the devils: since she it is who tames and crushes them. He thus expresses his thought: "The most blessed Virgin rules over the infernal regions. She is therefore called the ruling mistress of the devils, because she brings them into subjection." ‖ For this reason Mary is said in

* Prov. xxxi. 11.   † *De Laud. B. M.* l. 6.
‡ Ecclus. xxiv. 18.   § *Bibl. Marian.*
‖ *Pro Fest. V. M.* s. 3, a. 2, c. 2.

the sacred Canticles to be " terrible " to the infernal powers " as an army in battle array ; " * and she is called thus terrible because she well knows how to array her power, her mercy, and her prayers, to the discomfiture of her enemies, and for the benefit of her servants who in their temptations have recourse to her most powerful aid.

" As the vine I have brought forth a pleasant odor." † Thus does the Holy Ghost make Mary speak in the Book of Ecclesiasticus. " We are told," says St. Bernard on this passage, that " all venomous reptiles fly from flowering vines ; " ‡ for, as poisonous reptiles fly from flowering vines, so do devils fly from those fortunate souls in whom they perceive the perfume of devotion to Mary. And therefore she also calls herself, in the same book, a cedar : " I was exalted like a cedar in Libanus." § Not only because Mary was untainted by sin, as the cedar is incorruptible, but also, as Cardinal Hugo remarks on the foregoing text, because, " like the cedar, which by its odor keeps off worms, so also does Mary by her sanctity drive away the devils."

In Judea victories were gained by means of the ark. Thus it was that Moses conquered his enemies, as we learn from the Book of Numbers. " And when the ark was lifted up, Moses said : Arise, O Lord, and let Thy enemies be scattered." ‖ Thus was Jericho conquered ; thus also the Philistines ; " for the ark of God was there." ¶ It is well known that this ark was a figure of Mary. Cornelius à Lapide says, " In time of danger, Christians should fly to the most blessed Virgin, who contained Christ as manna in the ark of

* Cant. vi. 3.   † Ecclus. xxiv. 23.   ‡ *In Cant.* s. 60.
§ Ecclus. xxiv. 17.   ‖ Num. x. 35.   ¶ 1 Kings xiv. 18.

her womb, and brought Him forth to be the food and salvation of the world." For as manna was in the ark, so is Jesus (of Whom manna was a figure) in Mary; and by means of this ark we gain the victory over our earthly and infernal enemies. "And thus," St. Bernardine of Siena well observes, "that when Mary, the ark of the New Testament, was raised to the dignity of Queen of heaven, the power of hell over men was weakened and dissolved." *

Oh, how the infernal spirits tremble at the very thought of Mary and of her august name! says St. Bonaventure. "Oh, how fearful is Mary to the devils !" The saint compares these enemies to those of whom Job speaks: "He diggeth through houses in the dark: if the morning suddenly appear, it is to them the shadow of death." † Thieves go and rob houses in the dark; but as soon as morning dawns they fly, as if they beheld the shadow of death. "Precisely thus," in the words of the same saint, "do the devils enter a soul in the time of darkness;" meaning when the soul is in the obscurity of ignorance. They dig through the house of our mind when it is in the darkness of ignorance. But then, he adds, "if suddenly they are overtaken by the dawn, that is, if the grace and mercy of Mary enters the soul, its brightness instantly dispels the darkness, and puts the infernal enemies to flight, as if they fled from death." ‡ Oh, blessed is he who always invokes the beautiful name of Mary in his conflicts with hell !

In confirmation of this, it was revealed to St. Bridget "that God had rendered Mary so powerful over the devils that as often as they assault a devout

* *Pro Fest. V. M.* s. 12, a. 1, c. 3.
† Job xxiv. 16.   ‡ *Spec. B. V. lect.* 3, 11.

client who calls on this most blessed Virgin for help
she at a single glance instantly terrifies them, so that
they fly far away, preferring to have their pains redoubled rather than see themselves thus subject to
the power of Mary."*

The divine Bridegroom, when speaking of this His
beloved bride, calls her a lily: "As the lily is amongst
the thorns, so is My beloved amongst the daughters." †
On these words Cornelius à Lapide makes the reflection, "that as the lily is a remedy against serpents
and venomous things, so is the invocation of Mary a
specific by which we may overcome all temptations,
and especially those against purity, as all find who
put it in practice."

St. John Damascene used to say, "While I keep
my hope in thee unconquerable, O Mother of God, I
shall be safe. I will fight and overcome my enemies
with no other buckler than thy protection and thy
all-powerful aid." ‡ And all who are so fortunate as
to be the servants of this great Queen can say the
same thing. O Mother of God, if I hope in thee, I
most certainly shall not be overcome; for, defended
by thee, I will follow up my enemies, and oppose them
with the shield of thy protection and thy all-powerful
help; and then without doubt I shall conquer. For,
says St. James the monk (who was a doctor amongst
the Greeks), addressing Our Lord on the subject of
Mary, "Thou, O Lord, hast given us in Mary arms
that no force of war can overcome, and a trophy never
to be destroyed." §

It is said in the Old Testament, that God guided
His people from Egypt to the land of promise, "by

day in a pillar of a cloud, and by night in a pillar of fire." * This stupendous pillar, at times as a cloud, at others as fire, says Richard of St. Laurence, was a figure of Mary fulfilling the double office she constantly exercises for our good: as a cloud she protects us from the ardor of divine justice; and as fire she protects us from the devils. "Behold the twofold object for which Mary is given to us: to shelter us, as a cloud, from the heat of the sun of justice, and, as fire, to protect us against the devil." † She protects us as a burning fire: for, St. Bonaventure remarks, "as wax melts before the fire, so do the devils lose their power against those souls who often remember the name of Mary, and devoutly invoke it; and still more so if they also endeavor to imitate her virtues." ‡

The devils tremble even if they only hear the name of Mary. St. Bernard declares that in "the name of Mary every knee bows; and that the devils not only fear but tremble at the very sound of that name." § And as men fall prostrate with fear if a thunderbolt falls near them, so do the devils if they hear the name of Mary. Thomas à Kempis thus expresses the same sentiment: "The evil spirits greatly fear the Queen of heaven, and fly at the sound of her name as if from fire. At the very sound of the word Mary they are prostrated as by thunder." ∥

Oh, how many victories have the clients of Mary gained by only making use of her most holy name! It was thus that St. Anthony of Padua was always victorious; thus the Blessed Henry Suso; thus so many other lovers of this great Queen conquered.

---

* Exod. xiii. 21.   † *De Laud. B. Virg.* l. 7.
‡ *Spec. B. M. V.* lect. 3.
§ *Apud Lyræum, Tris. Mar.* l. 3, t. 9.   ∥ *Ad Nov.* s. 23.

We learn from the history of the missions in Japan that many devils appeared under the form of fierce animals to a certain Christian, to alarm and threaten him; but he thus addressed them: "I have no arms that you can fear; and if the Most High permits it, do whatever you please with me. In the meantime, however, I take the holy names of Jesus and Mary for my defence." At the very sound of these tremendous names the earth opened, and the proud spirits cast themselves headlong into it. St. Anselm declares that he himself "knew and had seen and heard many who had invoked the name of Mary in time of danger, and were immediately delivered from it." *

"Glorious indeed, and admirable," exclaims St. Bonaventure, "is thy name, O Mary; for those who pronounce it at death need not fear all the powers of hell;" † for the devils on hearing that name instantly fly, and leave the soul in peace. The same saint adds, "that men do not fear a powerful hostile army as much as the powers of hell fear the name and protection of Mary." ‡ "Thou, O Lady," says St. Germanus, "by the simple invocation of thy most powerful name, givest security to thy servants against all the assaults of the enemy." § Oh, were Christians but careful in their temptations to pronounce the name of Mary with confidence, never would they fall; for, as Blessed Allan remarks, "at the very sound of these words, Hail, Mary! Satan flies, and hell trembles." Our blessed Lady herself revealed to St. Bridget that the enemy flies even from the most abandoned sinners, and who consequently are the farthest from God, and fully possessed by the devil, if they only invoke her

* *De Excell. Virg.* c. 6.   † *Psalt. B. V. ps.* cx.
‡ *Spec. B. M. V.* lect. 3.   § *De Zona Deip.*

most powerful name with a true purpose of amendment. "All devils on hearing this name of Mary, filled with terror, leave the soul." But at the same time Our Lady added, "that if the soul does not amend and obliterate its sins by sorrow, the devils almost immediately return and continue to possess it."

Prayer.

Behold at thy feet, O Mary my hope, a poor sinner who has so many times been by his own fault the slave of hell. I know that by neglecting to have recourse to thee, my refuge, I allowed myself to be overcome by the devil. Had I always had recourse to thee, had I always invoked thee, I certainly should not have fallen. I trust, O Lady most worthy of all our love, that through thee I have already escaped from the hands of the devil, and that God has pardoned me. But I tremble lest at some future period I may again fall into the same bonds. I know that my enemies have not lost the hope of again overcoming me, and already they prepare new assaults and temptations for me. Ah, my Queen and refuge, do thou assist me. Place me under thy mantle; permit me not again to become their slave. I know that thou wilt help me and give me the victory, provided I invoke thee; but I dread lest in my temptations I may forget thee, and neglect to do so. The favor, then, that I seek of thee, and which thou must grant me, O most holy Virgin, is that I may never forget thee, and especially in time of temptation; grant that I may then repeatedly invoke thee, saying, "O Mary, help me; O Mary, help me." And when my last struggle with hell comes, at the moment of death, ah, then, my Queen, help me more than ever, and thou thyself remind me to call on thee more frequently either with my lips or in my heart; that, being thus filled with confidence, I may expire with thy sweet name and that of thy Son Jesus on my lips; that so I may be able to bless thee and praise thee, and not depart from thy feet in paradise for all eternity. Amen.

CHAPTER V.

Ad te suspiramus, gementes et flentes in hac lacrymarum valle.

TO THEE DO WE SIGH, MOURNING AND WEEPING, IN
THIS VALLEY OF TEARS.

MARY, OUR MEDIATRESS.

I. The Necessity of the Intercession of Mary for our Salvation.

THAT it is not only lawful but useful to invoke and
pray to the saints, and more especially to the Queen
of saints, the most holy and ever-blessed Virgin Mary,
in order that they may obtain us the divine grace, is an
article of faith, and has been defined by general coun-
cils, against heretics who condemned it as injurious to
Jesus Christ, who is our only mediator; but if a Jeremias after his death prayed for Jerusalem, * if the an-
cients of the Apocalypse presented the prayers of the
saints to God, † if a St. Peter promises his disciples
that after his death he will be mindful of them, ‡ if a
holy Stephen prays for his persecutors, § if a St. Paul
prays for his companions, ‖ if, in fine, the saints can
pray for us, why cannot we beseech the saints to intercede for us? St. Paul recommends himself to the

---

* 2 Mach. xv. 14. † Apoc. v. 8.
‡ 2 Pet. i. 15. § Acts vii. 59.
‖ Acts xxvii. 24; Eph. ii. 16; Phil. i. 4; Col. i. 3.

prayers of his disciples: "Brethren, pray for us." * St. James exhorts us to pray for one another: "Pray one for another, that you may be saved." † Then we can do the same.

No one denies that Jesus Christ is our only mediator of justice, and that He by His merits has obtained our reconciliation with God. But, on the other hand, it is impious to assert that God is not pleased to grant graces at the intercession of His saints, and more especially of Mary His Mother, whom Jesus desires so much to see loved and honored by all. Who can pretend that the honor bestowed on a mother does not redound to the honor of the son? "The glory of children are their fathers." ‡ Whence St. Bernard says, "Let us not imagine that we obscure the glory of the Son by the great praise we lavish on the Mother; for the more she is honored the greater is the glory of her Son." "There can be no doubt," says the saint, "that whatever we say in praise of the Mother is equally in praise of the Son." § And St. Ildephonsus also says, "That which is given to the Mother redounds to the Son; the honor given to the Queen is honor bestowed on the King." ‖ There can be no doubt that by the merits of Jesus Mary was made the mediatress of our salvation; not indeed a mediatress of justice, but of grace and intercession; as St. Bonaventure expressly calls her, "Mary, the most faithful mediatress of our salvation." ¶ And St. Laurence Justinian asks, "How can she be otherwise than full of grace, who has been made the ladder to paradise, the gate of heaven, the most true mediatress between God and man?" **

* I Thess. v. 25.   † James v. 16.   ‡ Prov. xvii. 6.
§ *De Laud. V. M. hom.* 4.   ‖ *De Virginit. S. M.* c. 12.
¶ *Spec. B. V. M.* lect. 9.   ** *S. in Ann. B. M.*

Hence the learned Suarez justly remarks, that if we implore our blessed Lady to obtain us a favor, it is not because we distrust the divine mercy, but rather that we fear our own unworthiness and the absence of proper dispositions; and we recommend ourselves to Mary, that her dignity may supply for our lowliness. He says that we apply to Mary "in order that the dignity of the intercessor may supply for our misery. Hence, to invoke the aid of the most blessed Virgin is not diffidence in the divine mercy, but dread of our own unworthiness." *

That it is most useful and holy to have recourse to the intercession of Mary can only be doubted by those who have not faith. But that which we intend to prove here is, that the intercession of Mary is even necessary to salvation ; we say necessary—not absolutely, but morally. This necessity proceeds from the will itself of God that all graces that He dispenses should pass through the hands of Mary, according to the opinion of St. Bernard, and which we may now with safety call the general opinion of theologians and learned men. The author of the "Reign of Mary" positively asserts that such is the case. It is maintained by Vega, Mendoza, Paciucchelli, Segneri, Poiré, Crasset, and by innumerable other learned authors. Even Father Natalis Alexander, who always uses so much reserve in his propositions, even he says that it is the will of God that we should expect all graces through the intercession of Mary. I will give his own words: " God wills that we should obtain all good things that we hope for from Him through the powerful intercession of the Virgin Mother, and we shall obtain them whenever (as we are in duty bound) we invoke her." † In confirma-

* *De Inc.* p. 2, d. 23, s. 3.   † *Ep.* 50 *in calce Theol.*

tion of this, he quotes the following celebrated passage of St. Bernard: "Such is God's will, that we should have all through Mary." * Father Contenson is also of the same opinion; for, explaining the words addressed by Our Lord on the cross to St. John: "Behold thy Mother," † he remarks, "that it is the same thing as if He had said: As no one can be saved except through the merits of My sufferings and death, so no one will be a partaker of the blood then shed otherwise than through the prayer of My Mother. He alone is a son of My sorrows who has Mary for his Mother. My wounds are ever-flowing fountains of grace; but their streams will reach no one but by the channel of Mary. In vain will he invoke Me as a Father who has not venerated Mary as a Mother. And thou, my disciple John, if thou lovest Me, love her; for thou wilt be beloved by Me in proportion to thy love for her." ‡

This proposition (that all that we receive from Our Lord comes through Mary) does not exactly please a certain modern writer, § who, although in other respects he speaks of true and false devotion with much learning and piety, yet when he treats of devotion towards the divine Mother he seems to grudge her that glory which was given her without scruple by a St. Germanus, a St. Anselm, a John Damascene, a St. Bonaventure, a St. Antoninus, a St. Bernardine, the Venerable Abbot of Celles, and so many other learned

---

* *De Aquæd.*   † John xix. 27.

‡ *Theol. mentis et cord.* t. 2, l. 10, d. 4, c. 1.

§ This author is the celebrated Muratori. An anonymous writer having attacked St. Alphonsus on the subject of the reproach directed here against Muratori, and of the doctrine maintained in this chapter, the saint sent him a reply which will be found at the end of "The Glories of Mary." —ED.

men, who had no difficulty in affirming that the intercession of Mary is not only useful, but necessary. The
same author says that the proposition that God grants
no grace otherwise than through Mary, is hyperbolical
and exaggerated, having dropped from the lips of
some saints in the heat of fervor, but which, correctly
speaking, is only to be understood as meaning that
through Mary we receive Jesus Christ, by whose merits
we obtain all graces : for he adds, " To believe that
God can grant us no graces without the intercession of
Mary, would be contrary to faith and the doctrine of
St. Paul, who says that we acknowledge but " one God
and one Mediator of God and men, the man Christ
Jesus." *

But with his leave, and going upon his own admis-
sions, meditation of justice by way of merit is one
thing, and meditation by grace by way of prayer is another. And again, it is one thing to say that God
cannot, and another that He will not, grant graces
without the intercession of Mary. We willingly admit
that God is the source of every good, and the absolute
master of all graces ; and that Mary is only a pure
creature, who receives whatever she obtains as a pure
favor from God. But who can ever deny that it is
most reasonable and proper to assert that God, in
order to exalt this great creature, who more than all
others honored and loved Him during her life, and
whom, moreover, He had chosen to be the Mother of
His Son, our common Redeemer, wills that all graces
that are granted to those whom He has redeemed should
pass through and be dispensed by the hands of Mary ?
We most readily admit that Jesus Christ is the only

* 1 Tim. ii. 5.

Mediator of justice, according to the distinction just made, and that by His merits He obtains us all graces and salvation ; but we say that Mary is the mediatress of grace ; and that receiving all she obtains through Jesus Christ, and because she prays and asks for it in the name of Jesus Christ, yet all the same whatever graces we receive, they come to us through her intercession.

There is certainly nothing contrary to faith in this, but the reverse. It is quite in accordance with the sentiments of the Church, which, in its public and approved prayers, teaches us continually to have recourse to this divine Mother, and to invoke her as the "health of the weak, the refuge of sinners, the help of Christians, and as our life and hope." In the office appointed to be said on the feasts of Mary, this same holy Church, applying the words of Ecclesiasticus to the Blessed Virgin, gives us to understand that in her we find all hope. " In me is all hope of life and of virtue ! " * In Mary is every grace. " In me is all grace of the way and of the truth." † In Mary, finally, we shall find life and eternal salvation : " Who finds me finds life, and draws salvation from the Lord." ‡ And elsewhere : " They that work by me shall not sin ; they that explain me shall have everlasting life." § And surely such expressions as these sufficiently prove that we require the intercession of Mary.

Moreover, we are confirmed in this opinion by so many theologians and Fathers, of whom it is certainly incorrect to say, as the above-named author does, that, in exalting Mary, they spoke hyperbolically and allowed great exaggerations to fall from their lips. To

* Ecclus. xxiv. 25.   † *Ib.*
‡ Prov. viii. 35.   § Ecclus. xxiv. 30, 31.

exaggerate and speak hyperbolically is to exceed the limits of truth ; and surely we cannot say that saints who were animated by the spirit of God, which is truth itself, spoke thus. If I may be allowed to make a short digression, and give my own sentiment, it is, that when an opinion tends in any way to the honor of the most blessed Virgin, when it has some foundation, and is not repugnant to the faith, nor to the decrees of the Church, nor to truth, the refusal to hold it, or to oppose it because the reverse may be true, shows little devotion to the Mother of God. Of the number of such as these I do not choose to be, nor do I wish my reader to be so, but rather of the number of those who fully and firmly believe all that can without error be believed of the greatness of Mary, according to the Abbot Rupert, who, amongst the acts of homage most pleasing to this good Mother, places that of firmly believing all that redounds to her honor. If there was nothing else to take away our fear of exceeding in the praises of Mary, St. Augustine * should suffice ; for he declares that whatever we may say in praise of Mary is little in comparison with that which she deserves, on account of her dignity of Mother of God ; and, moreover, the Church says, in the Mass appointed for her festivals, " Thou art happy, O sacred Virgin Mary, and most worthy of all praise." †

But let us return to the point, and examine what the saints say on the subject. St. Bernard says "that God has filled Mary with all graces, so that men may receive by her means, as by a channel, every good thing that comes to them." He says that " she is a full aqueduct, that others may receive of her plenitude." On this the saint makes the following signifi-

* *Serm.* 208, *E. B. app.*   † *M. Vot. a Nat.—Resp.* 7.

cant remark : " Before the birth of the Blessed Virgin, a constant flow of graces was wanting, because this acqueduct did not exist." * But now that Mary has been given to the world, heavenly graces constantly flow through her on all.

The devil, like Holofernes, who, in order to gain possession of the city of Bethulia, ordered the aqueducts to be destroyed, exerts himself to his utmost to destroy devotion to the Mother of God in souls ; for if this channel of grace is closed, he easily gains possession of them. And here, continues the same St. Bernard, " See, O souls, with what tender devotion Our Lord wills that we should honor Our Queen, by always having recourse to her protection ; and by relying on it ; for in Mary He has placed the plenitude of every good, so that henceforward we may know and acknowledge that whatever hope, grace, or other advantage we possess, all comes from the hand of Mary." † St. Antoninus says the same thing : " All graces that have ever been bestowed on men, all came through Mary." ‡ And on this account she is called the moon, according to the following remark of St. Bonaventure : " As the moon, which stands between the sun and the earth, transmits to this latter whatever it receives from the former, so does Mary pour out upon us who are in this world the heavenly graces that she receives from the divine Sun of justice." §

Again, the holy Church calls her " the happy gate of heaven " ; for as the same St. Bernard remarks : " As every mandate of grace that is sent by a king passes through the palace-gates, so does every grace that comes from heaven to the world pass through the

---

* *De Aquæd.*   † *De Aquæd.*
‡ P. 4, tit. 15, c. 20, § 12.   § *Spann. Polyanth. litt. M.* t. 6.

hands of Mary." * St. Bonaventure says that Mary is called "the gate of heaven, because no one can enter that blessed kingdom without passing through her." †

An ancient author, probably St. Sophronius, in a sermon on the Assumption, published with the works of St. Jerome, says "that the plenitude of grace which is in Jesus Christ came into Mary, though in a different way " ; meaning that it is Our Lord, as in the head, from which the vital spirits (that is, divine help to obtain eternal salvation) flow into us, who are the members of His mystical body ; and that the same plenitude is in Mary, as in the neck, through which these vital spirits pass to the members. The same idea is confirmed by St. Bernardine of Siena, who explains it more clearly, saying, "that all graces of the spiritual life that descend from Christ, their head, to the faithful, who are His mystical body, are transmitted through the instrumentality of Mary." The same St. Bernardine endeavors to assign a reason for this when he says, "that as God was pleased to dwell in the womb of this holy Virgin, she acquired, so to speak, a kind of jurisdiction over all graces ; for when Jesus Christ issued forth from her most sacred womb, all the streams of divine gifts flowed from her as from a celestial ocean." Elsewhere, repeating the same idea in more distinct terms, he asserts that "from the moment that the Virgin Mother conceived the divine Word in her womb, she acquired a special jurisdiction, so to say, over all the gifts of the Holy Ghost, so that no creature has since received any grace from God otherwise than through the hands of Mary." ‡

* *Apud. S. Bernardin, Pro Fest. V. M.* s. 5, c. 8.
† *In Luc.* i.   ‡ *Pro Fest. V. M.* s. 5, c. 8.

Another author, in a commentary on a passage of Jeremias, in which the prophet, speaking of the Incarnation of the Eternal Word, and of Mary His Mother, says that "a woman shall compass a man," * remarks, that " as no line can be drawn from the centre of a circle without passing by the circumference, so no grace proceeds from Jesus, who is the centre of every good thing, without passing by Mary, who compassed Him when she received Him into her womb." †

St. Bernardine says that for this reason " all gifts, all virtues, and all graces are dispensed by the hands of Mary to whomsoever, when, and as she pleases." ‡ Richard of St. Laurence also asserts " that God wills that whatever good things He bestows on His creatures should pass through the hands of Mary." § And therefore the venerable Abbot of Celles exhorts all to have recourse to " this treasury of graces " (for so he calls her); for the world and the whole human race have to receive every good that can be hoped for through her alone. " Address yourself to the Blessed Virgin," he says ; " for by her, and in her, and with her, and from her, the world receives, and is to receive, every good." ‖

It must now be evident to all that when these saints and authors tell us in such terms that all graces come to us through Mary, they do not simply mean to say that we " received Jesus Christ, the source of every good, through Mary," as the before named writer pretends ; but that they assure us that God, who gave us Jesus Christ, wills that all graces that have been, that are, and will be dispensed to men to the end of the world through the merits of Christ, should be dis-

* Jer. xxxi. 22.   † *Crasset, Vér. Dév.* p. 1. tr. 1, q. 5. § 2.
‡ *Pro Fest. V. M.* s. 5, c. 8.   § *De Laud. B. M.* l. 2, p. 3.
‖ *Cont. de V. M. in prol.*

pensed by the hands and through the intercession of Mary.

And thus Father Suarez concludes, that it is the sentiment of the universal Church, "that the intercession and prayers of Mary are, above those of all others, not only useful, but necessary." * Necessary, in accordance with what we have already said, not with an absolute necessity; for the mediation of Jesus Christ alone is absolutely necessary; but with a moral necessity; for the Church believes with St. Bernard, that God has determined that no grace shall be granted otherwise than by the hands of Mary. "God wills," says the saint, "that we should have nothing that has not passed through the hands of Mary;" † and before St. Bernard, St. Ildephonsus asserted the same thing, addressing the Blessed Virgin in the following terms: "O Mary, God has decided on committing all good gifts that He has provided for men to thy hands, and therefore He has intrusted all treasures and riches of grace to thee." ‡ And therefore St. Peter Damian remarks, "that God would not become man without the consent of Mary; in the first place, that we might feel ourselves under great obligations to her; and in the second, that we might understand that the salvation of all is left to the care of the Blessed Virgin." §

St. Bonaventure, on the words of the prophet Isaias, "And there shall come forth a rod out of the root of Jesse, and a flower shall rise up out of his root, and the spirit of the Lord shall rest upon him," ‖ makes a beautiful remark, saying: "Whoever desires the sevenfold grace of the Holy Spirit, let him seek for the

* *De Inc.* p. 2, d. 23, s. 3.
† *In Vig. Nat. D.* s. 3.   ‡ *In Cor. Virg.* c. 15.
§ *Paciucch. in Ps.* lxxxvi. *exc.* 1.   ‖ Is. xi. 1.

flower of the Holy Ghost in the rod." That is, for Jesus in Mary ; " For by the rod we find the flower, and by the flower, God." * And in the twelfth chapter of the same work, he adds, " If you desire to possess this flower, bend down the rod, which bears the flower, by prayer ; and so you will obtain it." The seraphical Father, in his sermon for the Epiphany, on the words of St. Matthew, " They found the child, with Mary His Mother," † reminds us, that if we wish to find Jesus we must go to Mary. We may, then, conclude, that in vain shall we seek for Jesus, unless we endeavor to find Him with Mary. ‡

And so St. Ildephonsus says, " I desire to be the servant of the Son; but because no one will ever be so without serving the Mother, for this reason I desire the servitude of Mary." §

Prayer.

O my soul, see what a sure hope of salvation and eternal life Our Lord has given thee, by having in His mercy inspired thee with confidence in the patronage of His Mother; and this, notwithstanding that so many times by thy sins thou hast merited His displeasure and hell. Thank thy God, and thank thy protectress Mary, who has condescended to take thee under her mantle; for of this thou mayest be well convinced, after the many graces that thou hast received by her means. Oh, yes, I do thank thee, my most loving Mother, for all thou hast done for me who am deserving of hell. And from how many dangers hast thou not delivered me O Queen! How many inspirations and mercies hast thou not obtained for me from God! What service what honor, have I ever rendered thee, that thou shouldst do so much

---

* *Spec. B. M. V.* lect. 6, 12.   † Matt. ii. 11.
‡ *Spann. Polyanth. litt. M.* t. 6.   § *De Virginit. Mar.* c. 12.

for me? I know that it is thy sole goodness that has impelled thee. Ah, too little would it be in comparison with all that I owe thee, did I shed my blood and give my life for thee; for thou hast delivered me from eternal death; thou hast enabled me, as I hope, to recover divine grace; to thee, in fine, I owe all I have. My most amiable Lady, I, poor wretch that I am, can make thee no return but that of always loving and praising thee. Ah, disdain not to accept the tender affection of a poor sinner, who is inflamed with love for thy goodness. If my heart is unworthy to love thee, because it is impure and filled with earthly affections, it is thou who must change it. Ah, change it, then. Bind me to my God, and bind me so that I may never more have it in my power to separate myself from His love. Thou askest of me that I should love thy God, and I ask of thee that thou shouldst obtain this love for me, to love Him always; this is all that I desire. Amen.

II. The same subject continued.

St. Bernard says, "that as a man and a woman cooperated in our ruin, so it was proper that another man and another woman should cooperate in our redemption, and these two were Jesus and His Mother Mary." "There is no doubt," says the saint, "that Jesus Christ alone was more than sufficient to redeem us; but it was more becoming that both sexes should cooperate in the reparation of an evil in causing which both had shared."* Hence Blessed Albert the Great calls Mary, the "helper of redemption;"† and the Blessed Virgin herself revealed to St. Bridget, that "as Adam and Eve sold the world for an apple, so did she with her Son redeem it as it were with one heart."‡ This is confirmed by St. Anselm, who

---

In Sign. Magn.   † *Super Miss.*q. 29, § 3.
‡ Rev. l. 1, c. 35.

says, "that although God could create the world out of nothing, yet, when it was lost by sin, he would not repair the evil without the cooperation of Mary." *

Suarez says,† "that Mary cooperated in our salvation in three ways ; first, by having merited by a merit of congruity the Incarnation of the Word ; secondly, by having continually prayed for us whilst she was living in this world ; thirdly, by having willingly sacrificed the life of her Son to God." For this reason Our Lord has justly decreed, that as Mary cooperated in the salvation of man with so much love, and at the same time gave such glory to God, so all men through her intercession are to obtain their salvation.

Mary is called " the cooperator in our justification ;" for to her God has intrusted all graces intended for us ;‡ and therefore St. Bernard affirms, "that all men, past, present, and to come, should look upon Mary as the means and negotiator of the salvation of all ages." §

Jesus Christ says, that no one can find Him unless the eternal Father first draws him by the means of divine grace: " No one comes to Me unless My Father draws him." ‖ Thus also does Jesus address His Mother, says Richard of St. Laurence : "No one comes to Me unless My Mother first of all draws him by her prayers." ¶ Jesus was the fruit of Mary, as St. Elizabeth told her: " Blessed art thou amongst women, and blessed is the fruit of thy womb." ** Whoever, therefore, desires the fruit must go to the tree ; whoever desires Jesus must go to Mary; and whoever finds Mary will most certainly find Jesus.

* *Orat.* 51.   † *De Inc.* p. 2, d. 23, s. 1.   ‡ *Marial.* p. 3, s. 1.
  § *In Pent.* s. 2.   ‖ John vi. 44.
  ¶ *De Laud. B. M.* 1. 12, *p.* 2.   ** Luke i. 42.

When St. Elizabeth saw that the most blessed Virgin had come to visit her in her own house, not knowing how to thank her, and filled with humanity, she exclaimed: " And whence is this to me, that the Mother of my Lord should visit me ?" * But how could this be ? we may ask. Did not St. Elizabeth already know that not only Mary, but also Jesus, had entered her house ? Why then does she say that she is unworthy to receive the Mother, and not rather, that she is unworthy to receive the Son, who had come to visit her ? Ah, yes, it was that the saint knew full well that when Mary comes she brings Jesus, and therefore it was sufficient to thank the Mother without naming the Son.

" She is like the merchant's ship, she bringeth her bread from afar." † Mary was this fortunate ship that brought us Jesus Christ from heaven, who is the living bread that comes down from heaven to give us eternal life, as He Himself says: " I am the living bread which came down from heaven : if any man eat of this bread, he shall live forever." ‡ And hence Richard of St. Laurence says, " that in the sea of this world all will be lost who are not received into this ship; that is to say, all who are not protected by Mary ; " and therefore he adds, " As often as we see ourselves in danger of perishing in the midst of the temptations and contending passions of this life, let us have recourse to Mary, and cry out quickly, O Lady, help us, save us, if thou wilt not see us perish." §

Remark, by the by, that this writer does not scruple to address these words to Mary : " Save us, we perish ; " as does a certain author already noticed, and who says,

* Luke i. 43.   † Prov. xxxi. 14.
‡ John vi. 51.   § *De Laud. B. M.* l. 11, c. 8.

that we cannot ask Mary to save us, as this belongs to
God alone.   But since a culprit condemned to death
can beg a royal favorite to save him by interceding
with the king that his life may be spared, why cannot
we ask the Mother of God to save us by obtaining us
eternal life?   St. John Damascene scrupled not to
address her in these words : " Pure and immaculate
Virgin, save me, and deliver me from eternal damnation." *   St. Bonaventure calls Mary " the salvation
of those who invoke her."   The holy Church ap-
proves of the invocation by also calling her the " salvation of the weak."   And shall we scruple to ask
her to save us, when " the way of salvation is open to
none otherwise than through Mary " ? † as a certain
author remarks.   And before him St. Germanus had
said the same thing, speaking of Mary : " No one is
saved but through thee." ‡

But let us now see what else the saints say of the
need in which we are of the intercession of the divine
Mother.   The glorious St. Cajetan used to say, that
we may seek for graces, but shall never find them
without the intercession of Mary.   This is confirmed
by St. Antoninus, who thus beautifully expresses himself : " Whoever asks and expects to obtain graces
without the intercession of Mary, endeavors to fly
without wings ; " § for, as Pharao said to Joseph,
" the land of Egypt is in thy hands," and addressed all
who came to him for food to Joseph, " Go to Joseph," ‖
so does God sent us to Mary when we seek for grace :
" Go to Mary ; " for " He has decreed," says St. Bernard, " that He will grant no graces otherwise than by

* *Paracl. in Deip.*   † *Paciucch. In Ps.* lxxxvi. *exc.* I
‡ *De Zona Deip.*   § P. 4, tit. 15, c. 22, § 9.
                    ‖ Gen. xli. 55.

the hands of Mary." *   " And thus," says Richard of
St. Laurence, " our salvation is in the hands of Mary ;
so that we Christians may with much greater reason
say of her than the Egyptians of Joseph, ' Our salvation is in thy hands.' " †   The venerable Raymond
Jordano repeats the same thing : " Our salvation is in
her hands." ‡   Cassian speaks in still stronger terms.
He says absolutely, " that the salvation of all depends
on their being favored and protected by Mary." §   He
who is protected by Mary will be saved ; he who is
not will be lost.   St. Bernardine of Siena thus addresses the Blessed Virgin : " O Lady, since thou art
the dispenser of all graces, and since the grace of salvation can only come through thy hands, our salvation
depends on thee." ‖

Therefore, Richard of St. Laurence had good reason for saying, that " as we should fall into the abyss
if the ground were withdrawn from under our feet, so
does a soul deprived of the succor of Mary first fall into
sin and then into hell." ¶   St. Bonaventure says, that
" God will not save us without the intercession of
Mary."   And that " as a child cannot live without a
nurse to suckle it, so no one can be saved without the
protection of Mary."   Therefore he exhorts us " to
thirst after devotion to her, to preserve it with care,
and never to abandon it until we have received her
maternal blessing in heaven." **   " And whoever,"
exclaims St. Germanus, " could know God, were it not
for thee, O most holy Mary ? who could be saved ?
who would be preserved from dangers ? who would

---

* *De Aquæd.*   †(Gen. xlvii. 25.)—*De Laud. B. M.* l. 2, c. 1.
‡ *Cont. de V. in prol.*   § *Pelbart, Stell.* l. 12, p. 1, a. 3.
‖ *Pro Fest. V. M.* s. 13, a. 2, c. 3.
¶ *De Laud. B. M.* l. 8.   ** *Cant. in Psalt.*

receive any grace, were it not for thee, O Mother of God, O full of grace?"

The following are the beautiful words in which he expresses himself: "There is no one, O most holy Mary, who can know God but through thee; no one who can be saved or redeemed but through thee, O Mother of God; no one who can be delivered from dangers but through thee, O Virgin Mother; no one who obtains mercy but through thee, O filled with all grace!" And in another place, addressing her, he says: "No one would be free from the effects of the concupiscence of the flesh and from sin, unless thou didst open the way to him." *

And as we have access to the Eternal Father, says St. Bernard, only through Jesus Christ, so have we access to Jesus Christ only through Mary: "By thee we have access to the Son, O blessed finder of grace, bearer of life, and Mother of salvation, that we may receive Him by thee, who through thee was given to us." † This is the reason given by the saint why Our Lord has determined that all shall be saved by the intercession of Mary; and therefore he calls her the Mother of grace and of our salvation.

"Then," asks St. Germanus, "what will become of us? what hope can we have of salvation, if thou dost abandon us, O Mary, who art the life of Christians?" ‡

"But," says the modern author already quoted, "if all graces come through Mary, when we implore the intercession of other saints, they must have recourse to the mediation of Mary. But that," he says, "no one believes or ever dreamed."

As to believing it, I reply that in that there can be

* *In Dorm. V. M.* s. 2.   † *De Adv. Dom.* s. 2.
‡ *De Zona Deip.*

no error or difficulty. What difficulty can there be in saying that God, in order to honor His Mother, and having made her Queen of saints, and willing that all graces shall be dispensed by her hands, should also will that the saints should address themselves to her to obtain favors for their clients?

And as to saying that no one ever dreamed of such a thing, I find that St. Bernard, St. Anselm, St. Bonaventure, Suarez, and others, expressly declare it to be the case. " In vain," says St. Bernard, " would a person ask other saints for a favor, if Mary did not interpose to obtain it." Some other author, explaining the words of the psalm, "All the rich among the people shall entreat thy countenance," * says, " that the saints are the rich of that great people of God, who, when they wish to obtain a favor from God for their clients, recommend themselves to Mary, and she immediately obtains it." And Father Suarez correctly remarks, " that we beg the saints to be our intercessors with Mary, because she is their Queen and sovereign Lady. Amongst the saints," he says, " we do not make use of one to intercede with the other, as all are of the same order; but we do ask them to intercede with Mary, because she is their sovereign and Queen." † And this is precisely what St. Benedict promised to St. Frances of Rome, as we read in Father Marchese ; for he appeared to her, and taking her under his protection, he promised that he would be her advocate with the divine Mother.

In confirmation of this, St. Anselm addresses our blessed Lady and says, " O Lady, whatever all the saints, united with thee, can obtain, thou canst obtain

* Ps. xliv. 13.   † *De Inc.* p. 2, d. 23, s. 3.

alone." "And why is this?" asks the saint; "why is it that thou alone hast such great power? Ah, it is because that thou alone art the Mother of our common Redeemer; thou art the spouse of God; thou art the universal Queen of heaven and earth. If thou dost not speak for us, no saint will pray for or help us. But if thou beginnest to pray for us, then will all the saints do the same and succor us." *

So that Father Segneri,† in his "Devout Client of Mary," applying with the Catholic Church the words of Ecclesiasticus to her, "I alone have compassed the circuit of heaven," ‡ says, that " as the first sphere by its motion sets all the others in motion, so it is when Mary prays for a soul; immediately the whole heavenly court begins to pray with her." "Nay, more," says St. Bonaventure, "whenever the most sacred Virgin goes to God to intercede for us, she, as Queen, commands all the angels and saints to accompany her, and unite their prayers to hers." §

And thus, finally, do we understand why the holy Church requires that we should salute and invoke the divine Mother under the glorious title of " our hope." The impious Luther said, " that he could not endure that the Roman Church should call Mary, who is only a creature, ' our hope ;' for," said he, " God alone, and Jesus Christ as our Mediator, is our hope : and God curses those who place their hope in a creature, according to the prophet Jeremias, ' Cursed be the man that trusteth in man.' " ‖ But the Church teaches us to invoke Mary on all occasions, and to call her " our hope ; hail, our hope ! " Whoever places his confidence in a creature independently of God, he

* *Orat.* 45.   † *Div. di M.* p. 1, c. 7, § 4.   ‡ Ecclus. xxiv. 8,
§ *Paciucch. Super Sal. Ang. exc.* 19.   ‖ Jer. xvii. 5.

certainly is cursed by God; for God is the only source and dispenser of every good, and the creature without God is nothing, and can give nothing. But if Our Lord had so disposed it, as we have already proved that He has done, that all graces should pass through Mary as by a channel of mercy, we not only can but ought to assert that she, by whose means we receive the divine graces, is truly our hope.

Therefore St. Bernard says, "that she is his greatest confidence, and the whole foundation of his hope." * St. John Damascene says the same thing; for he thus addresses the most blessed Virgin: "O Lady, in thee have I placed all my hope; and with my eyes fixed on thee, from thee do I expect salvation." † St. Thomas says, that "Mary is the whole hope of our salvation," ‡ and St. Ephrem, addressing her, says, "O most holy Virgin, receive us under thy protection, if thou wilt see us saved, for we have no hope of salvation but through thy means." §

Let us, then, in the words of St. Bernard, "endeavor to venerate this divine Mother with the whole affection of our hearts; for such is the will of God, who is pleased that we should receive every good thing from her hand." ‖ And therefore the saint exhorts us, whenever we desire or ask for any grace, to recommend ourselves to Mary, and to be assured that we shall receive it by her means; for, he says, if thou dost not deserve the favor from God, Mary, who will ask it for thee, will deserve to receive it; "because thou wast unworthy of the gift, it was bestowed on Mary, that through her thou mightest receive all that thou hast." ¶ The saint then advises us to recom-

---

* *De Aquæd.* † *Paracl. in Deip.* ‡ *Exp. in Sal. Ang.*
§ *De Laud. Dei gen.* ‖ *De Aquæd.* ¶ *In Vig. Nat. D.* s. 3.

mend all that we offer to God to the care of Mary, be
they good works or prayers, if we wish Our Lord to
accept them. "Whatever thou mayest offer to God,
be sure to recommend it to Mary, in order not to
meet with a repulse." *

Prayer.

O Queen and Mother of mercy, who dispenses graces
to all who have recourse to thee, with so much liberality,
because thou art a Queen, and with so much love, because
thou art our most loving Mother; to thee do I, who am
so devoid of merit and virtue, and so loaded with debts
to the divine Justice, recommend myself this day. O
Mary, thou holdest the keys of all the divine mercies; forget not my miseries, and leave me not in my poverty.
Thou art so liberal with all, and givest more than thou
art asked for, oh, be thus liberal with me. O Lady, protect me; this is all that I ask of thee. If thou protectest
me, I fear nothing. I fear not the evil spirits; for thou
art more powerful than all of them. I fear not my sins:
for thou by one word canst obtain their full pardon from
God. And if I have thy favor, I do not even fear an angry
God; for a single prayer of thine will appease Him. In
fine, if thou protectest me, I hope all; for thou art all-powerful. O Mother of mercy, I know that thou takest pleasure and dost glory in helping the most miserable, and,
provided they are not obstinate, that thou canst help
them. I am a sinner, but am not obstinate; I desire to
change my life. Thou canst, then, help me; oh, help me
and save me. I now place myself entirely in thy hands
Tell me what I must do in order to please God, and I am
ready for all, and hope to do all with thy help, O Mary—
Mary my Mother, my light, my consolation, my refuge,
my hope. Amen, amen, amen.

* *De Aquæd.*

CHAPTER VI.

Eia ergo, Advocata nostra!

O GRACIOUS ADVOCATE.

MARY, OUR ADVOCATE.

I. Mary is an Advocate who is able to save all.

So great is the authority that mothers possess over their sons, that even if they are monarchs, and have absolute dominion over every person in their kingdom, yet never can mothers become the subjects of their sons. It is true that Jesus now in heaven sits at the right hand of the Father, that is, as St. Thomas* explains it, even as man, on account of the hypostatical union with the Person of the divine Word. He has supreme dominion over all, and also over Mary; it will nevertheless be always true that for a time, when He was living in this world, He was pleased to humble Himself and to be subject to Mary, as we are told by St. Luke: "And He was subject to them."† And still more, says St. Ambrose, Jesus Christ having deigned to make Mary His Mother, inasmuch as He was her Son, He was truly obliged to obey her. And for this reason, says Richard of St. Laurence, " of other saints we say that they are with God ; but of Mary alone can it be said that she was so far favored

---

* *De Human. J. C. a.* 23.   † Luke ii. 51.

as to be not only herself submissive to the will of God, but even that God was subject to her will." And whereas of all other virgins, remarks the same author, we must say that " they follow the Lamb whithersoever He goeth," * of the Blessed Virgin Mary we can say that the Lamb followed her, having become subject to her.†

And here we say, that although Mary, now in heaven, can no longer command her Son, nevertheless her prayers are always the prayers of a mother, and consequently most powerful to obtain whatever she asks. " Mary," says St. Bonaventure, " has this great privilege, that with her Son she above all the saints is most powerful to obtain whatever she wills." ‡ And why ? Precisely for the reason on which we have already touched, and which we shall later on again examine at greater length, because they are the prayers of a mother.

Therefore, says St. Peter Damian, the Blessed Virgin can do whatever she pleases both in heaven and on earth. She is able to raise even those who are in despair to confidence ; and he addresses her in these words : " All power is given to thee in heaven and on earth, and nothing is impossible to thee who canst raise those who are in despair to the hope of salvation." And then he adds that " when the Mother goes to seek a favor for us from Jesus Christ " (whom the saint calls the golden altar of mercy, at which sinners obtain pardon), " her Son esteems her prayers so greatly, and is so desirous to satisfy her, that when she prays it seems as if she rather commanded than prayed, and was rather a queen than a handmaid." §

---

* Apoc. xiv. 4.　　　† *De Laud B. M.* l. i. c. 5.
‡ *Spec. B. M. V. lect.* 6.　　§ *In Nat. B. V.* s. 1.

Jesus is pleased thus to honor His beloved Mother, who honored Him so much during her life, by immediately granting all that she asks or desires. This is beautifully confirmed by St. Germanus, who addressing our blessed Lady says: " Thou art the Mother of God, and all-powerful to save sinners, and with God thou needest no other recommendation; for thou art the Mother of true life." *

" At the command of Mary, all obey, even God." St. Bernardine fears not to utter this sentence ; meaning, indeed, to say that God grants the prayers of Mary as if they were commands.† And hence St. Anselm addressing Mary says : " Our Lord, O most holy Virgin, has exalted thee to such a degree that by His favor all things that are possible to Him should be possible to thee." ‡ " For thy protection is omnipotent, O Mary," § says Cosmas of Jerusalem. " Yes, Mary is omnipotent," repeats Richard of St. Laurence; " for the queen by every law enjoys the same privileges as the king. And as," he adds, " the power of the son and that of the mother is the same, a mother is made omnipotent by an omnipotent son." ‖ " And thus," says St Antoninus, " God has placed the whole Church, not only under the patronage, but even under the dominion of Mary." ¶

Since the Mother, then, should have the same power as the Son, rightly has Jesus, who is omnipotent, made Mary also omnipotent ; though, of course, it is always true that where the Son is omnipotent by nature, the Mother is only so by grace. But that she is so is evident from the fact that whatever the Mother

---

* *In Dorm V. M.* s. 2. † *Pro Fest. V. M.* s. 5, c. 6.
‡ *De Excell. Virg.* c. 12. § *Hymn.* 6.
‖ *De Laud. B. M.* l. 4. ¶ P. 4, t. 15, c. 20, § 2.

asks for, the Son never denies her; and this was revealed to St. Bridget, who one day heard Jesus talking with Mary, and thus address her: "Ask of Me what thou wilt, for no petition of thine can be void." As if He had said, "My Mother, thou knowest how much I love thee; therefore ask all that thou wilt of Me; for it is not possible that I should refuse thee anything." And the reason that He gave for this was beautiful: "Because thou never didst deny Me anything on earth, I will deny thee nothing in heaven." * My Mother, when thou wast in the world, thou never didst refuse to do anything for the love of Me; and now that I am in heaven, it is right that I should deny thee nothing that thou askest. Mary, then, is called omnipotent in the sense in which it can be understood of a creature who is incapable of a divine attribute. She is omnipotent, because by her prayers she obtains whatever she wills.

With good reason, then, O great advocate, does St. Bernard say, "Thou willest, and all things are done." And St. Anselm: "Whatever thou, O Virgin, willest can never be otherwise than accomplished."† Thou willest, and all is done. If thou art pleased to raise a sinner from the lowest abyss of misery to the highest degree of sanctity, thou canst do it. Blessed Albert the Great, on this subject, makes Mary say: "I have to be asked that I may will; for if I will a thing, it is necessarily done."‡

Thus St. Peter Damian, reflecting on the great power of Mary, and begging her to take compassion on us, addresses her, saying: "Oh, let thy nature move thee, let thy power move thee; for the more thou art

* Rev. l. 6, c. 23; l. 1, c. 24.
† *Excell. V.* c. 12. ‡ *De Laud. B. M.* l. 2, c. 1.

powerful, the greater should thy mercy be." * O
Mary, our own beloved advocate, since thou hast so
compassionate a heart, that thou canst not even see
the wretched without being moved to pity, and since,
at the same time, thou hast so great power with God,
that thou canst save all whom thou dost protect,—
disdain not to undertake the cause of us poor miserable
creatures who place all our hope in thee. If our
prayers cannot move thee, at least let thine own benign heart do so; or, at least, let thy power do so,
since God has enriched thee with so great power, in
order that the richer thou art in power to help us, the
more merciful thou mayest be in the will to assist us.
But St. Bernard reassures us on this point; for he
says that Mary is as immensely rich in mercy as she
is in power; and that, as her charity is most powerful,
so also it is most clement and compassionate, and its
effects continually prove it to be so. He thus expresses himself: " The most powerful and merciful
charity of the Mother of God abounds in tender compassion and in effectual succor: it is equally rich in
both." †

From the time that Mary came into the world, her
only thought, after seeking the glory of God, was to
succor the miserable. And even then she enjoyed the
privilege of obtaining whatever she asked. This we
know from what occurred at the marriage feast of
Cana in Galilee. When the wine failed, the most
blessed Virgin, being moved to compassion at the
sight of the affliction and shame of the bride and
bridegroom, asked her Son to relieve them by a
miracle, telling Him that " they had no wine." Jesus

* *In Nat. B. V.* s. 1.   † *In Assumpt.*

answered : " Woman, what is that to thee and Me ? My hour is not yet come." * And here remark, that although Our Lord seemed to refuse His Mother the favor she asked, and said, What is it to thee, O woman, and to Me, if the wine has failed ? This is not the time for Me to work a miracle ; the time will be when I begin to preach, and when miracles will be required to confirm My doctrines. And yet Mary, as if the favor had already been granted, desired those in attendance to fill the jars with water, for they would be immediately satisfied. And so it was ; for Jesus, to content His Mother, changed the water into the best wine. But how was this ? As the time for working miracles was that of the public life of Our Lord, how could it be that, contrary to the divine decrees, this miracle was worked ? No ; in this there was nothing contrary to the decrees of God ; for though, generally speaking, the time for miracles was not come, yet from all eternity God had determined by another decree that nothing that she asked should ever be refused to the divine Mother. And therefore Mary, who well knew her privilege, although her Son seemed to have refused her the favor, yet told them to fill the jars with water, as if her request had already been granted. That is the sense in which St. John Chrysostom understood it ; for, explaining these words of Our Lord, " Woman, what is it to thee and Me ?" he says, that " though Jesus answered thus, yet in honor of His Mother He obeyed her wish." † This is confirmed by St. Thomas, who says that by the words, " My hour is not yet come," Jesus Christ intended to show, that had the request come from any other, He would not

* John ii. 3.   † *In Jo. hom.* 21.

then have complied with it ; but because it was addressed to Him by His Mother, He could not refuse
it. St. Cyril and St. Jerome, quoted by Barrada,*
say the same thing. Also Gandavensis, on the foregoing passage of St. John, says, that " to honor His
Mother, Our Lord anticipated the time for working
miracles." †

In fine, it is certain that no creature can obtain so
many mercies for us as this tender advocate, who is
thus honored by God, not only as His beloved handmaid, but also as His true Mother.   And thus, William
of Paris says, addressing her, " No creature can obtain
so many and so great favors as thou obtainest for poor
sinners ; and thus without doubt God honors thee not
only as a handmaid, but as His most true Mother." ‡
Mary has only to speak, and her Son executes all.
Our Lord conversing with the spouse in the sacred
Canticles,—that is Mary,—says, " Thou that dwellest
in the gardens, the friends hearken; make me hear thy
voice." §   The saints are the friends, and they, when
they seek a favor for their clients, wait for their Queen
to ask and obtain it; for, as we said in the fifth chapter, "no grace is granted otherwise than at the prayer
of Mary."   And how does Mary obtain favors?   She
has only to let her voice be heard,—" make me hear
thy voice."   She has only to speak, and her Son
immediately grants her prayer.   Listen to the Abbot
William explaining, in this sense, the above-mentioned
text.   In it he introduces the Son addressing Mary :
" Thou who dwellest in the heavenly gardens, intercede with confidence for whomsoever thou wilt; for
it is not possible that I should so far forget that I am

* T. ii. l. 3, c. 1. † *In Conc. Ev.* c. 18.
‡ *De Rhet. div.* c. 18. § Cant. viii. 13.

thy Son as to deny anything to thee, My Mother. Only let thy voice be heard ; for to be heard by a son is to be obeyed." * The Abbot Godfrey says, "that although Mary obtains favors by asking, yet she asks with a certain maternal authority, and therefore we ought to feel confident that she obtains all she desires and asks for us." †

Valerius Maximus, ‡ relates that when Coriolanus was besieging Rome, the prayers of his friends and all the citizens were insufficient to make him desist; but as soon as he beheld his mother Veturia imploring him, he could no longer refuse, and immediately raised the siege. But the prayers of Mary with Jesus are as much more powerful than those of Veturia as the love and gratitude of this Son for His most dear Mother are greater. Father Justin Micoviensis says that "a single sigh of the most blessed Mary can do more than the united suffrages of all the saints." § And this was acknowledged by the devil himself to St. Dominic, who, as it is related by Father Paciuc-chelli, ‖ obliged him to speak by the mouth of a pos-sessed person; and he said that "a single sigh from Mary was worth more before God than the united suf-frages of all the saints."

St. Antoninus says that "the prayers of the Blessed Virgin, being the prayers of a mother, have in them something of a command; so that it is impossible that she should not obtain what she asks."¶ St. Germanus, encouraging sinners to recommend themselves to this advocate, thus addresses her : "As thou hast, O Mary, the authority of a mother with God, thou obtainest

* *Paciucch. In Sal. Ang. exc.* 20.   † *In Fest. B. M.* s. 8.
‡ *Ex mir.* l. 5, c. 4.   § *Super Litan.* s. 270.
‖ *In Sal. Ang. exc.* 3.   ¶ *P.* 4. tit. 15, c. 17, § 4.

pardon for the most enormous sinners; since that
Lord in all things acknowledges thee as His true and
spotless Mother, He cannot do otherwise than grant
what thou askest." * And so it was that St. Bridget
heard the saints in heaven addressing our blessed
Lady : " O most blessed Queen, what is there that
thou canst not do ? Thou hast only to will, and it is
accomplished." † And this corresponds with that celebrated saying, " that which God can do by His power,
that thou canst do by prayer, O sacred Virgin."
" And perchance," says St. Augustine, "if it is unworthy of the benignity of the Lord to be thus jealous
of the honor of His Mother, who declares that He came
into the world, not to break, but to observe the law :
but this law commands us to honor our parents." ‡ St.
George, Archbishop of Nicomedia, says that Jesus
Christ, even as it were to satisfy an obligation under
which He placed Himself towards His Mother, when
she consented to give Him His human nature, grants
all she asks : " The Son, as if paying a debt, grants all
thy petitions." § And on this the holy martyr St. Methodius exclaims: " Rejoice, rejoice, O Mary, for thou
hast that Son thy debtor, who gives to all and receives
from none. We are all God's debtors for all that we
possess, for all is His gift; but God has been pleased
to become thy debtor in taking flesh from thee and becoming man." ‖

Therefore St. Augustine says, "that Mary, having
merited to give flesh to the divine Word, and thus
supply the price of our redemption, that we might be
delivered from eternal death ; therefore is she more

* *In Dorm. Deip.* s. 2.　　　† Rev. l. 4, c. 74.
‡ *Lib. de Assumpt. B. M.* c. 5.　　§ *Or. de Ingr. B. V.*
‖ *Or. de Sim. et Anna.*

powerful than all others to help us to gain eternal life." *　St. Theophilus, Bishop of Alexandria, in the time of St. Jerome, left in writing the following words : " The prayers of His Mother are a pleasure to the Son, because He desires to grant all that is granted on her account, and thus recompense her for the favor she did Him in giving Him His body." †　St. John Damascene, addressing the Blessed Virgin, says, " Thou, O Mary, being Mother of the most high God, canst save all by thy prayers, which are increased in value by the maternal authority." ‡

Let us conclude with St. Bonaventure, who, considering the great benefit conferred on us by Our Lord in giving us Mary for our advocate, thus addresses her : " O truly immense and admirable goodness of our God, which has been pleased to grant thee, O sovereign Mother, to us miserable sinners for our advocate, in order that thou, by thy powerful intercession, mayest obtain all that thou pleasest for us." " O wonderful mercy of our God," continues the same saint, " who in order that we might not fly on account of the sentence that might be pronounced against us, has given us His own Mother and the patroness of graces to be our advocate." §

Prayer.

I will address thee, O great Mother of God, in the words of St. Bernard : " Speak, O Lady, for thy Son heareth thee, and whatever thou askest thou wilt obtain." ‖ Speak, speak, then, O Mary, our advocate, in favor of us poor miserable creatures.　Remember that it was also for

---

* *Serm.* 208, *E. B. app.*　　† *Salazar. In Prov.* viii. 18.
‡ *Men. Græc,* 20 *Jan. ad Mat.*　§ *Stim. div. am.* p. 3, c. 19.
‖ *Depr. ad. gl. V.*

our good that thou didst receive so great power and so high a dignity. A God was pleased to become thy debtor by taking humanity of thee, in order that thou mightest dispense at will the riches of divine mercy to sinners. We are thy servants, devoted in a special manner to thee ; and I am one of these, I trust, even in a higher degree. We glory in living under thy protection. Since thou dost good to all, even to those who neither know nor honor thee, nay, more, to those who outrage and blaspheme thee, how much more may we not hope from thy benignity, which seeks out the wretched in order to relieve them, we who honor, love, and confide in thee ? We are great sinners, but God has enriched thee with compassion and power far exceeding our iniquities. Thou canst, and hast the will to save us ; and the greater our unworthiness, the greater shall be our hope in order to glorify thee the more in heaven, when by thy intercession we get there. O Mother of mercy, we present thee our souls, once cleansed and rendered beautiful in the blood of Jesus Christ, but, alas, since that time, defiled by sin. To thee do we present them ; do thou purify them. Obtain for us true conversion ; obtain for us the love of God, perseverance, heaven. We ask thee for much ; but what is it ? perhaps thou canst not obtain all ? Is it perhaps too much for the love God bears thee ? Ah, no ! for thou hast only to open thy lips and ask thy divine Son ; He will deny thee nothing. Pray, then, pray O Mary, for us, pray ; thou wilt certainly obtain all : and we shall with the same certainty obtain the kingdom of heaven.

II. Mary is so tender an Advocate that she does not refuse to defend the cause even of the most miserable.

So many are the reasons that we have for loving this our most loving Queen, that if Mary was praised throughout the world ; if in every sermon Mary alone was spoken of ; if all men gave their lives for Mary ; still all would be little in comparison with the homage and gratitude that we owe her in return for the tender love she bears to men, and even to the most miserable sinners who preserve the slightest spark of devotion for her.

Blessed Raymond Jordano, who, out of humility, called himself the Idiot, used to say, "that Mary knows not how to do otherwise than love those who love her ; and that even she does not disdain to serve those who serve her ; and in favor of such a one, should he be a sinner, she uses all her power in order to obtain his forgiveness from her blessed Son." And he adds, "that her benignity and mercy are so great, that no one, however enormous his sins may be, should fear to cast himself at her feet : for she never can reject any one who has recourse to her." "Mary, as our most loving advocate, herself offers the prayers of her servants to God, and especially those who are placed in her hands ; for as the Son intercedes for us with the Father, so does she intercede with the Son, and does not cease to make interest with both for the great affair of our salvation, and to obtain for us the graces we ask." *

With good reason, then, does Denis the Carthusian call the Blessed Virgin " the singular refuge of the lost, the hope of the most abandoned, and the advocate of all sinners who have recourse to her." †

But should there by chance be a sinner who, though not doubting her power, might doubt the compassion of Mary, fearing perhaps that she might be unwilling to help him on account of the greatness of his sins, let him take courage from the words of St. Bonaventure. " The great, the special privilege of Mary is,

* *Cont. de V. M. in prol.* † *De Laud. V.* I. 2, a. 23₁

that she is all-powerful with her Son." "But," adds the saint, "to what purpose would Mary have so great power if she cared not for us?" "No," he concludes, "let us not doubt, but be certain, and let us always thank Our Lord and His divine Mother for it, that in proportion as her power with God exceeds that of all the saints, so is she in the same proportion our most loving advocate, and the one who is the most solicitous for our welfare." *

"And who, O Mother of mercy," exclaims St. Germanus, in the joy of his heart, "who, after thy Jesus, is as tenderly solicitous for our welfare as thou art?" "Who defends us in the temptations with which we are afflicted as thou defendest us? Who, like thee, undertakes to protect sinners, fighting, as it were, in their behalf?" "Therefore," he adds, "thy patronage, O Mary, is more powerful and loving than anything of which we can ever form an idea." †

"For," says the Blessed Raymond Jordano, "whilst all the other saints can do more for their own clients than for others, the divine Mother, as Queen of all, is the advocate of all, and has a care for the salvation of all." ‡

Mary takes care of all, even of sinners; indeed she glories in being called in a special manner their advocate, as she herself declared to the venerable Sister Mary Villani, saying: "After the title of Mother of God, I rejoice most in that of advocate of sinners."

Blessed Amadeus says, "that our Queen is constantly before the Divine Majesty, interceding for us with her most powerful prayers." And as in heaven "she well knows our miseries and wants, she cannot

---

* *Spec. B. V. lect.* 6.   † *De Zona Deip.*
‡ *Cont. de V. M. in prol.*

do otherwise than compassionate us ; and thus, with the affection of a mother, moved to tenderness towards us, pitying and benign, she is always endeavoring to help and save us." * And therefore does Richard of St. Laurence encourage each one, however bad he may be, to have recourse with confidence to this sweet advocate, being assured that he will always find her ready to help him ; † " for," says the Abbot Godfrey, " Mary is always ready to pray for all." ‡

"Oh, with what efficacy and love," says St. Bernard, " does this good advocate interest herself in the affair of our salvation ! " § St. Bonaventure, considering the affection and zeal with which Mary intercedes for us with the Divine Majesty, in order that Our Lord may pardon us our sins, help us with His grace, free us from dangers, and relieve us in our wants, says, addressing the Blessed Virgin, in the words of an ancient writer : " We know that we have as it were but one solicitous in heaven for us, and thou art this one, so greatly does thy solicitude for us exceed that of all the saints." ‖ That is, " O Lady, it is true that all the saints desire our salvation, and pray for us ; but the love, the tenderness that thou showest us in heaven, in obtaining for us by thy prayers so many mercies from God, obliges us to acknowledge that in heaven we have but one advocate, and that is thyself ; and that thou alone art truly loving and solicitous for our welfare."

Who can ever comprehend the solicitude with which Mary constantly stands before God in our behalf ? "She is never weary of defending us," ¶ says St.

* *De Laud. V. hom.* 8.   † *De Laud. B. M.* 1, 2, p. 1.
‡ *In Fest. B. M.* s. 8.   § *In Assumpt.* s. 1.
‖ *Ap. S. Bonav. Spec. B. V.* l. 6.   ¶ *De Zona Deip.*

Germanus ; and the remark is beautiful, meaning that so great is the compassion excited in Mary by our misery, and such is the love that she bears us, that she prays constantly, and relaxes not her efforts in our behalf ; that by her prayers she may effectually defend us from evil, and obtain for us sufficient graces. "She has never done enough."

Truly unfortunate should we poor sinners be, had we not this great advocate, who is so powerful and compassionate, and at the same time "so prudent and wise, that the Judge, her Son," says Richard of St. Laurence, "cannot condemn the guilty who are defended by her." *   And therefore St. John Geometra salutes her, saying, "Hail, O court, for putting an end to litigation." †   For all causes defended by this most wise advocate are gained.

For this reason is Mary called, by St. Bonaventure, "the wise Abigail." ‡   This is the woman we read of in the First Book of Kings, who by her beautiful supplications knew so well how to appease King David when he was indignant against Nabal ; and indeed so far as to induce him to bless her, in gratitude for having prevented him, by her sweet manners, from avenging himself on Nabal with his own hand.§ This is exactly what Mary constantly does in heaven, in favor of innumerable sinners : by her tender and unctuous prayers she knows so well how to appease the divine justice, that God Himself blesses her for it, and, as it were, thanks her for having withheld Him from abandoning and chastising them as they deserved.

"On this account it was," says St. Bernard, "that the Eternal Father, wishing to show all the mercy

* *De Laud. B. M.* l. 2, p. 1.   † *In V. Deip. Hymn.* 4.
‡ *Laus B. M.* n. 13.   § 1 Kings xxv. 33.

possible, besides giving us Jesus Christ, our principal
advocate with Him, was pleased also to give us Mary,
as our advocate with Jesus Christ." " There is no
doubt," the saint adds, " that Jesus Christ is the only
mediator of justice between men and God ; that, by
virtue of His own merits and promises, He will and
can obtain us pardon and the divine favors ; but because men acknowledge and fear the divine majesty,
which is in Him as God, for this reason it was necessary to assign us another advocate, to whom we might
have recourse with less fear and more confidence, and
this advocate is Mary, than whom we cannot find one
more powerful with His divine Majesty, or one more
merciful towards ourselves." The saint says, "Christ
is a faithful and powerful mediator between God and
men, but in Him men fear the majesty of God. A
mediator, then, was needed with the mediator Himself;
nor could a more fitting one be found than Mary."

" But," continues the same saint, " should any one
fear to go to the feet of this most sweet advocate, who
has nothing in her of severity, nothing terrible, but
who is all courteous, amiable, and benign, he would
indeed be offering an insult to the tender compassion
of Mary." And he adds, " Read, and read again, as
often as you please, all that is said of her in the Gos-
pels, and if you can find the least trait of severity recorded of her, then fear to approach her. But no,
this you can never find; and therefore go to her with
a joyful heart, and she will save you by her intercession." *

How beautiful is the exclamation put in the mouth
of a sinner who has recourse to Mary, by William of

* *In Sign. Magn.*

Paris! "O most glorious Mother of God, I, in the miserable state to which I am reduced by my sins, have recourse to thee, full of confidence, and if thou rejectest me, I remind thee that thou art in a way bound to help me, since the whole Church of the faithful calls thee and proclaims thee the Mother of mercy." "Thou, O Mary, art that one who, from being so dear to God, art always listened to favorably. Thy great compassion was never wanting to any one; thy most sweet affability never despised any sinner that recommended himself to thee, however great his sins." And what! Perhaps falsely, and for nothing, the whole Church calls thee its advocate, and the refuge of sinners. "Never, O my Mother, let my sins prevent thee from fulfilling the great office of charity which is thine, and by which thou art, at the same time, our advocate and a mediatress of peace between men and God, and who art, after thy Son, our only hope, and the secure refuge of the miserable. All that thou possessest of grace and glory, and the dignity even of Mother of God, so to speak, thou owest to sinners, for it was on their account that the divine Word made thee His Mother. Far be it from this divine Mother, who brought the source itself of tender compassion into the world, to think that she should ever deny her mercy to any sinner who has recourse to her. Since, then, O Mary, thy office is to be the peace-maker between God and men, let thy tender compassion, which far exceeds all my sins, move thee to succor me." *

"Be comforted then, O you who fear," will I say with St. Thomas of Villanova; "breathe freely and take courage, O wretched sinners; this great virgin,

* *De Rhet. div.* c. 18.

who is the Mother of your Son and Judge, is also the
advocate of the whole human race; fit for this office,
for she can do what she wills with God; most wise,
for she knows all the means of appeasing Him;
universal, for she welcomes all, and refuses to defend
no one."*

Prayer.

O great Mother of my Lord, I see full well that my ingratitude towards God and thee, and this too for so many
years, has merited for me that thou shouldst justly
abandon me, and no longer have a care of me, for an ungrateful soul is no longer worthy of favors. But I, O
Lady, have a high idea of thy great goodness; I believe
it to be far greater than my ingratitude. Continue, then,
O refuge of sinners, and cease not to help a miserable
sinner who confides in thee. O Mother of mercy, deign
to extend a helping hand to a poor fallen wretch who asks
thee for pity. O Mary, either defend me thyself, or tell
me to whom I can have recourse, and who is better able
to defend me than thou, and where I can find with God a
more clement and powerful advocate than thou, who art
His Mother. Thou, in becoming the Mother of Our
Saviour, wast thereby made the fitting instrument to save
sinners, and wast given me for my salvation. O Mary,
save him who has recourse to thee. I deserve not thy
love, but it is thine own desire to save sinners, that makes
me hope that thou lovest me. And if thou lovest me,
how can I be lost? O my own beloved Mother, if by
thee I save my soul, as I hope to do, I shall no longer be
ungrateful, I shall make up for my past ingratitude, and
for the love which thou hast shown me, by my everlasting
praises, and all the affections of my soul. Happy in
heaven, where thou reignest, and wilt reign forever, I
shall always sing thy mercies, and kiss for eternity those
loving hands which have delivered me from hell, as often

* *Dial.* l. 7, c. 35.

as I have deserved it by my sins. O Mary, my liberator, my hope, my Queen, my advocate, my own sweet Mother, I love thee ; I desire thy glory, and I love thee forever. Amen, amen. Thus do I hope.

III. Mary is the Peace-maker between Sinners and God.

The grace of God is the greatest and the most desirable of treasures for every soul. It is called by the Holy Ghost an infinite treasure ; for by the means of divine grace we are raised to the honor of being the friends of God. These are the words of the Book of Wisdom : " For she is an infinite treasure to men ; which they·that use become the friends of God."* And hence Jesus, our Redeemer and God, did not hesitate to call those His friends who were in grace : " You are My friends."† O accursed sin, that dissolves this friendship ! " But your iniquities," says the prophet Isaias, " have divided between you and your God." ‡ And putting hatred between the soul and God, it is changed from a friend into an enemy of its Lord, as expressed in the Book of Wisdom : " But to God the wicked and his wickedness are hateful alike." §

What, then, must a sinner do who has the misfortune to be the enemy of God ? He must find a mediator who will obtain pardon for him, and who will enable him to recover the lost friendship of God. " Be comforted, O unfortunate soul, who hast lost thy God," says St. Bernard ; " thy Lord Himself has provided thee with a mediator, and this is His Son Jesus, who can obtain for thee all that thou desirest. He has given thee Jesus for a mediator ; and what is there that such a Son cannot obtain from the Father ? " ‖

---

* Wis. vii. 14.   † John xv. 14.   ‡ Is. lix. 2.
§ Wis. xiv. 9.   ‖ *De Aquæd.*

But, O God, exclaims the saint, and why should this merciful Saviour, who gave His life to save us, be ever thought severe? Why should men believe Him terrible who is all love? O distrustful sinners, what do you fear? If your fear arises from having offended God, know that Jesus has fastened all your sins on the cross with His own lacerated hands, and having satisfied divine justice for them by His death, He has already effaced them from your souls. Here are the words of the saint : " They imagine Him rigorous, who is all compassion ; terrible, who is all love. What do you fear, O ye of little faith ? With His own hands He has fastened your sins to the cross." * " But if by chance," adds the saint, " thou fearest to have recourse to Jesus Christ because the majesty of God in Him overawes thee—for though He became man, He did not cease to be God—and thou desirest another advocate with this divine mediator, go to Mary, for she will intercede for thee with the Son, who will most certainly hear her ; and then He will intercede with the Father, who can deny nothing to such a Son." Thence St. Bernard concludes, "this divine Mother, O my children, is the ladder of sinners, by which they reascend to the height of divine grace : she is my greatest confidence, she is the whole ground of my hope." †

The Holy Ghost, in the sacred Canticles, makes the most blessed Virgin use the following words : " I am a wall ; and my breasts are as a tower, since I am become in his presence as one finding peace ; "‡ that is, I am the defender of those who have recourse to me, and my mercy towards them is like a tower of refuge, and therefore I have been appointed by my Lord the

In Cant. s. 38.   † *De Aquæd.*   ‡ Cant. viii. 10.

peace-maker between sinners and God. "Mary," says Cardinal Hugo, on the above text, "is the great peace-maker, who finds and obtains the reconciliation of enemies with God, salvation for those who are lost, pardon for sinners, and mercy for those who are in despair." And therefore was she called by the divine bridegroom, "beautiful as the curtains of Solomon." * In the tents of David, questions of war alone were treated ; but in those of Solomon, questions of peace only were entertained ; and thus does the Holy Spirit give us to understand that the Mother of mercy never treats of war and vengeance against sinners, but only of peace and forgiveness for them.

Mary was prefigured by the dove which returned to Noe in the Ark with an olive-branch in its beak,† as a pledge of the peace which God granted to men. And on this idea St. Bonaventure thus addresses our blessed Lady : "Thou art that most faithful dove; thou wast a sure mediatress between God and the world, lost in a spiritual deluge;" ‡ thou, by presenting thyself before God, hast obtained for a lost world peace and salvation. Mary, then, was the heavenly dove which brought to a lost world the olive-branch, the sign of mercy, since she in the first place gave us Jesus Christ, who is the source of mercy; and then, by His merits, obtained all graces for us. § "And as by Mary," says St. Epiphanius, "heavenly peace was once for all given to the world,‖ so by her are sinners still reconciled to God." Wherfore Blessed Albert the Great makes her say : "I am that dove of

---

* Cant. i. 4.   † Gen. viii. 11.
‡ *Spec. B. M. V. lect.* 9.   § *Spinelli, Mar. Deip.* c. 16.
‖ *Hom. in Laud. B. M.*

Noe, which brought the olive-branch of universal peace to the Church." *

Again, the rainbow seen by St. John, which encircled the throne of God, was an express figure of Mary : " And there was a rainbow round about the throne." † It is thus explained by Cardinal Vitalis : " The rainbow round the throne is Mary, who softens the judgment and sentence of God against sinners ;" ‡ meaning, that she is always before God's tribunal, mitigating the chastisements due to sinners.　St. Bernardine of Siena says, " that it was of this rainbow that God spoke when He promised Noe that He would place it in the clouds as a sign of peace, that on looking at it He might remember the eternal peace which He had covenanted to man."　" I will set My bow in the clouds, and it shall be the sign of a covenant between Me and between the earth . . . and I shall see it, and shall remember the everlasting covenant." §　" Mary," says the saint, " is this bow of eternal peace ; " ‖　" for, as God on seeing it remembers the peace promised to the earth, so does He, at the prayers of Mary, forgive the crimes of sinners, and confirm His peace with them." ¶

For the same reason Mary is compared to the moon in the sacred Canticles : " Fair as the moon." ** " For," says St. Bonaventure, " as the moon is between the heavens and the earth, so does Mary continually place herself between God and sinners in order to appease Our Lord in their regard, and to enlighten them to return to Him." ††

The chief office given to Mary, on being placed in

---

* *Bibl. Mar. Cant.* 16.　　　　† *Apoc.* iv. 3.
‡ *Spec. S. Script. de B. V. M.*　§ *Gen.* ix. 13.
‖ *Pro Fest. S. M.* s. 1, a. 1, c. 3.　¶ *In Apoc.* iv.
** *Cant.* vi. 9.　　　　†† *Spann. Polyanth.* litt. M. t. 6.

this world, was to raise up souls that had fallen from divine grace, and to reconcile them with God. " Feed thy goats," * was Our Lord's command to her in creating her. It is well known that sinners are understood by goats, and that as at the last judgment, the just, under the figure of sheep, will be on the right hand, so will the goats be on the left. " These goats," says the Abbot William, " are intrusted to thee, O great Mother, that thou mayest change them into sheep ; and those who by their sins deserve to be driven to the left, will by thy intercession be placed on the right." And therefore Our Lord revealed to St. Catherine of Siena, " that He had created this His beloved daughter to be as a most sweet bait by which to catch men, and especially sinners, and draw them to God." † But on this subject we must not pass over the beautiful reflection of William the Angelical on the above text of the sacred Canticles, in which he says, " that God recommended ' her own' goats to Mary ; for," adds this author, " the Blessed Virgin does not save all sinners, but those only who serve and honor her. So much so indeed, that those who live in sin, and neither honor her with any particular act of homage, nor recommend themselves to her in order to extricate themselves from sin, they certainly are not Mary's goats, but at the last judgment, for their eternal misery, will be driven to the left hand with the damned."

A certain nobleman, despairing of his salvation on account of his many crimes, was encouraged by a monk to have recourse to the most blessed Virgin, and for this purpose to visit a venerated statue of Mary

* Cant. i. 7.　　　　　　　† *Dial.* c. 139.

in a particular church. He went there, and, on seeing the image, he felt as if she invited him to cast himself at her feet and to have confidence. He hastened
to prostrate himself and kiss her feet, when Mary extended her hand, gave it him to kiss, and on it he
saw written these words : " I will deliver thee from
those who oppress thee "; as though she had said, my
son, despair not, for I will deliver thee from the sins
and sorrows that weigh so heavily on thee. On reading these sweet words, this poor sinner was filled with
such sorrow for his sins, and, at the same time, with so
ardent a love for God and His tender Mother, that he
instantly expired at the feet of Mary.

Oh, how many obstinate sinners does not this loadstone of hearts draw each day to God ! For thus did
she call herself one day, saying to St. Bridget, " As
the loadstone attracts iron, so do I attract hearts." *
Yea, even the most hardened hearts, to reconcile
them with God. We must not suppose that such
prodigies are extraordinary events ; they are every-
day occurrences. For my own part, I could relate
many cases of the kind that have occurred in our
missions, where certain sinners with hearts harder
than iron, continued so through all the other sermons,
but no sooner did they hear the one on the mercies of
Mary, than they were filled with compunction and returned to God. St. Gregory † says that the unicorn is
so fierce a beast, that no hunter can take it ; at the
voice only of a virgin crying out, will this beast approach, and without resistance allow itself to be bound
by her. Oh, how many sinners, more savage than the
wild beasts themselves, and who fly from God, at the

* Rev. l. 3, c. 32.   † *Moral.* l. 31, c. 13.

voice of the Virgin Mary approach and allow themselves to be sweetly bound to God by her!

St. John Chrysostom says, "that another purpose for which the Blessed Virgin Mary was made the Mother of God was, that she might obtain salvation for many who, on account of their wicked lives, could not be saved according to the rigor of divine justice, but might be so with the help of her sweet mercy and powerful intercession." This is confirmed by St. Anselm, who says, "that Mary was raised to the dignity of Mother of God rather for sinners than for the just, since Jesus Christ declares that He came to call not the just, but sinners." * For this reason, the holy Church sings: "Thou dost not abhor sinners, without whom thou wouldst never have been worthy of such a Son." † For the same reason William of Paris, invoking her, says : "O Mary, thou art obliged to help sinners for all the gifts, the graces, and high honors which are comprised in the dignity of Mother of God that thou hast received ; thou owest all, so to say, to sinners ; for on their account thou wast made worthy to have a God for thy Son." ‡ "If then, Mary," concludes St. Anselm, "was made Mother of God on account of sinners, how can I, however great my sins may be, despair of pardon?" §

The holy Church tells us, in the prayer said in the Mass of the vigil of the Assumption, "that the divine Mother was taken from this world that she might interpose for us with God, with certain confidence of obtaining all." Hence St. Justin calls Mary an arbitratrix. "The eternal Word uses Mary," he says,

---

* *De Excell. V.* c. 1.   † *Crasset Vér. Dév.* p. 1, tr. 1, q. 10.
‡ *De Rhet div.*c. 18.   § *De Excell. V.* c. 1.

"as an arbitratrix." * An arbitrator is one to whose hands contending parties confide their whole case ; and so the saint meant to say, that as Jesus is the mediator with the Eternal Father, so also is Mary our mediatress with Jesus ; and that He puts all the reasons that He has for pronouncing sentence against us into her hands.

St. Andrew of Crete calls Mary "a pledge, a security for our reconciliation with God." † That is, that God goes about seeking for reconciliation with sinners by pardoning them ; and in order that they may not doubt of their forgiveness, He has given them Mary as a pledge of it, and therefore he exclaims, "Hail, O peace of God with men ! " ‡ Wherefore St. Bonaventure encourages a sinner, saying : " If thou fearest that on account of thy faults God in His anger will be avenged, what hast thou to do ? Go, have recourse to Mary, who is the hope of sinners ; and, if thou fearest that she may refuse to take thy part, know that she cannot do so, for God Himself has imposed on her the duty of succoring the miserable." § The Abbot Adam also says, " Need that sinner fear being lost to whom the Mother of the Judge offers herself to be Mother and advocate ? " " And thou, O Mary," he adds, " who art the Mother of mercy, wilt thou disdain to intercede with thy Son, who is the Judge, for another son, who is a sinner ? Wilt thou refuse to interpose in favor of a redeemed soul, with the Redeemer who died on a cross to save sinners ? " ‖ No, no, thou wilt not reject him, but with all affection thou wilt pray for all who have recourse to thee, well

---

* *Expos. Fid. de Trin.*   † *In Dorm. B. V.* s. 2.
‡ *In Deip. Annunt.*   § *Stim. div. am.* p. 3, c. 12.
‖ *Marial.* s. 1,

knowing that "that Lord who has appointed thy Son a mediator of peace between God and man, has also made thee mediatress between the Judge and the culprit." *

"Then, O sinner," says St. Bernard, "whoever thou mayest be, imbedded in crime, grown old in sin, despair not; thank thy Lord, who, that He might show thee mercy, has not only given His Son for thy advocate, but, to encourage thee to greater confidence, has provided thee with a mediatress who by her prayers obtains whatever she wills.† Go then, have recourse to Mary, and thou wilt be saved."

Prayer.

O my most sweet Lady, since thy office is, as William of Paris says, that of a mediatress between God and sinners,‡ I will address thee in the words of St. Thomas of Villanova: "Fulfil thy office in my behalf, O tender advocate; do thy work." § Say not that my cause is too difficult to gain; for I know, and all tell me so, that every cause, no matter how desperate, if undertaken by thee, is never, and never will be, lost. And will mine be lost? Ah, no, this I cannot fear. The only thing that I might fear is, that, on seeing the multitude of my sins, thou mightest not undertake my defence. But, on seeing thy immense mercy, and the very great desire of thy most sweet heart to help the most abandoned sinners, even this I cannot fear. And who was ever lost that had recourse to thee? Therefore I invoke thy aid, O my great advocate, my refuge, my hope, my mother Mary. To thy hands do I entrust the cause of my eternal salvation. To thee do I commit my soul; it was lost, but thou hast to save it. I will always thank Our Lord for having given me this great confidence in thee; and which, notwith-

* *Marial.* s. 1.   † *In Sign. Magn.*
‡ *De Rhet. Div.* c. 18.   § *In Nat. B. V. con.* 3.

standing my unworthiness, I feel is an assurance of salvation. I have but one fear to afflict me, O beloved Queen, and that is, that I may one day, by my own negligence, lose this confidence in thee. And therefore I implore thee, O Mary, by the love thou bearest to Jesus, thyself to preserve and increase in me more and more this sweet confidence in thy intercession, by which I hope most certainly to recover the divine friendship, that I have hitherto so madly despised and lost; and having recovered it, I hope, through thee, to preserve it; and preserving it by the same means, I hope at length to thank thee for it in heaven, and there to sing God's mercies and thine for all eternity. Amen. This is my hope; thus may it be, thus will it be.

CHAPTER VII.

Illos tuos misericordes oculos ad nos converte.

TURN, THEN, THINE EYES OF MERCY TOWARDS US.

MARY, OUR GUARDIAN.

Mary is all eyes to pity and succor us in our Necessities.

ST. EPIPHANIUS calls the divine Mother many-eyed,[*] indicating thereby her vigilance in assisting us poor creatures in this world. A possessed person was once being exorcised, and was questioned by the exorcist as to what Mary did. The devil replied, " She descends and ascends." And he meant, that this benign Lady is constantly descending from heaven to bring graces to men, and re-ascending to obtain the divine favor on our prayers. With reason, then, used St. Andrew Avellino to call the Blessed Virgin the " Heavenly Commissioner," for she is continually carrying messages of mercy, and obtaining graces for all, for just and sinners. God fixes His eyes on the just, says the royal prophet. " The eyes of the Lord are on the just." [†] " But the eyes of the Lady," says Richard of St. Laurence, " are on the just and on the sinners." " For," he adds, " the eyes of Mary are the eyes of a mother ; and a mother not only watches

---

[*] *Hom. in Laud. S. M.*   [†] Ps. xxxiii. 16.

her child to prevent it from falling, but when it has
fallen, she raises it up." *

Jesus Himself revealed this to St. Bridget, for one
day He allowed her to hear Him thus addressing His
holy Mother : " My Mother, ask Me what thou wilt." †
And thus is her Son constantly addressing Mary in
heaven, taking pleasure in gratifying His beloved
Mother in all that she asks. But what does Mary
ask ? St. Bridget heard her reply : " I ask mercy for
sinners." ‡ As if she had said, " My Son, Thou hast
made me the Mother of mercy, the refuge of sinners,
the advocate of the miserable ; and now thou tellest
me to ask what I desire ; what can I ask except
mercy for them ? I ask mercy for the miserable."

" And so, O Mary, thou art so full of mercy," says
St. Bonaventure, with deep feeling, " so attentive in
relieving the wretched, that it seems that thou hast no
other desire, no other anxiety." § And as amongst
the miserable, sinners are the most miserable of all,
Venerable Bede declares " that Mary is always praying to her Son for them."

" Even whilst living in this world," says St. Jerome,
" the heart of Mary was so filled with tenderness and
compassion for men, that no one ever suffered so
much for his own pains as Mary suffered for the pains
of others." The compassion for others in affliction
she well showed at the marriage-feast of Cana, spoken
of in the preceding chapters, when, the wine failing,
without being asked, remarks St. Bernardine of Siena,
she charged herself with the office of a tender comfortress ; ‖ and moved to compassion at the sight of

* *De Laud. B. M.* l. 2, p. 2.   † *Lib.* vi. *cap.* 23.
‡ Rev. l. I., c. 50.   § *Stim. div. am.* p. 3, c. 19.
‖ *Pro Fest. V. M.* s. 9, a. 3, c. 2.

the embarrassment of the bride and bridegroom, she interposed with her Son, and obtained the miraculous change of water into wine.

"But perhaps," says St. Peter Damian, addressing Mary, "now that thou art raised to the high dignity of Queen of heaven, thou forgettest us poor creatures?" "Ah, far be such a thought from our minds," he adds; "for it would little become the great compassion that reigns in the heart of Mary ever to forget such misery as ours." * The proverb, that "honors change our manners," does not apply to Mary. With worldlings it is otherwise; for they, when once raised to a high dignity, become proud, and forget their former poor friends, but it is not so with Mary, who rejoices in her own exaltation, because she is thus better able to help the miserable.

On this subject St. Bonaventure applies to the Blessed Virgin the words addressed to Ruth: "Blessed art thou of the Lord, my daughter, and thy latter kindness has surpassed the former;" † meaning to say, "that if the compassion of Mary was great towards the miserable when living in this world, it is much greater now that she reigns in heaven." He then gives the reason for this, saying, "that the divine Mother shows, by the innumerable graces that she obtains for us, her greater mercy; for now she is better acquainted with our miseries." Then he adds, that as the splendor of the sun surpasses that of the moon, so does the compassion of Mary, now that she is in heaven, surpass the compassion she had for us when in the world." In conclusion he asks: "Who is there living in this world who does not enjoy the light of the sun? and on whom does not the mercy of Mary shine?" ‡

* *In Nat. B. V.* s. 1. † Ruth iii. 10. ‡ *Spec. B. V.* lect. 10.

For this reason, in the sacred Canticles, she is called "bright as the sun." * "For no one is excluded from the warmth of this sun," says St. Bonaventure, according to the words of the Psalmist ; † and the same thing was also revealed to St. Bridget, by St. Agnes, who told her, " that our Queen, now that she is united to her Son in heaven, cannot forget her innate goodness; and therefore she shows her compassion to all, even to the most impious sinners ; so much so, that, as the celestial and terrestrial bodies are all illumined by the sun, so there is no one in the world, who, if he asks for it, does not, through the tenderness of Mary, partake of the divine mercy." ‡

A great sinner, in the kingdom of Valencia, who, having become desperate, and, in order not to fall into the hands of justice, had determined on becoming a Mahometan, was on the point of embarking for the purpose, when, by chance, he passed before a church in which Father Jerome Lopez was preaching on the mercy of God. On hearing the sermon he was converted, and made his confession to the Father, who asked him whether he had ever practised any devotion, on account of which God might have shown him so great mercy ; he replied, that his only devotion was a prayer to the Blessed Virgin, in which he daily begged her not to abandon him. In an hospital the same Father found a sinner, who had not been to confession for fifty-five years ; and the only devotion he practised was, that when he saw an image of Mary he saluted her, and begged that she would not allow him to die in mortal sin. He then told him, that on an occasion, when fighting with an enemy, his sword was

* Cant. vi. 9.   † Ps. xviii. 7.   ‡ Rev. l. 3, c. 30.

broken; and, turning to our blessed Lady, he cried out: "Oh, I shall be killed and lost for eternity; Mother of sinners, help me." Scarcely had he said the words than he found himself transported to a place of safety. After making a general confession he died, full of confidence.*

St. Bernard says, " that Mary has made herself all to all, and opens her merciful heart to all, that all may receive of her fulness ; the slave redemption, the sick health, those in affliction comfort, the sinner pardon, and God glory ; that thus there may be no one who can hide himself from her warmth."† " Who can there be in the world," exclaims St. Bonaventure, " who refuses to love this most amiable Queen ? She is more beautiful than the sun, and sweeter than honey. She is a treasure of goodness, amiable and courteous to all." " I salute thee, then," continues the enraptured saint, " O my Lady and Mother, nay, even my heart, my soul. Forgive me, O Mary, if I say that I love thee ; for if I am not worthy to love thee, at least thou art all-worthy to be loved by me."

It was revealed to St. Gertrude,‡ that when these words are addressed with devotion to the most blessed Virgin, " Turn, then, O most gracious advocate, thine eyes of mercy towards us," Mary cannot do otherwise than yield to the demand of whoever thus invokes her.

" Ah, truly, O great Lady," says St. Bernard, " does the immensity of thy mercy fill the whole earth."§ " And therefore," says St. Bonaventure, " this loving Mother has so earnest a desire to do good to all, that not only is she offended by those who positively outrage her (as some are wicked enough to do), but she

---

* *Patrign. Menol.* 2. *Feb.*   † *In Sign. Magn.*
‡ *Insin.* l. 4, c. 53.   § *In Assumpt.* s. 4.

is offended at those who do not ask her for favors or graces." So that St. Idelbert addresses her, saying : " Thou, O Lady, teachest us to hope for far greater graces than we deserve, since thou never ceasest to dispense graces far, far beyond our merits." *

The prophet Isaias foretold that, together with the great work of the redemption of the human race, a throne of divine mercy was to be prepared for us poor creatures : " And a throne shall be prepared in mercy." † What is this throne ? St. Bonaventure answers, " Mary is this throne, at which all—just and sinners—find the consolations of mercy." He then adds : " For as we have a most merciful Lord, so also we have a most merciful Lady. Our Lord is plenteous in mercy to all who call upon Him, and Our Lady is plenteous in mercy to all who call upon her." ‡ As Our Lord is full of mercy, so also is Our Lady ; and as the Son knows not how to refuse mercy to those who call upon Him, neither does the Mother. Wherefore the Abbot Guerric thus addresses the Mother, in the name of Jesus Christ : " My Mother, in thee will I establish the seat of my government ; through thee will I pronounce judgments, hear prayers, and grant the graces asked of me. Thou hast given me my human nature, and I will give thee my divine nature," § that is, omnipotence, by which thou mayest be able to help to save all whomsoever thou pleasest.

One day, when St. Gertrude was addressing the foregoing words, " Turn thine eyes of mercy towards us," to the divine Mother, she saw the Blessed Virgin pointing to the eyes of her Son, whom she held in her arms, and then said, " These are the most compassion-

---

* *Ep.* 20, *Bibl. Patr.*   † Is. xvi. 5.
‡ *Spec. B. M. V.* lect. 9.   § *De Assumpt.* s. 2.

ate eyes that I can turn for their salvation towards all who call upon me." *

A sinner was once weeping before an image of Mary, imploring her to obtain pardon for him from God, when he perceived that the Blessed Virgin turned towards the child that she held in her arms, and said, "My Son, shall these tears be lost?" And he understood that Jesus Christ had already pardoned him. †

How, then, is it possible that any one can perish who recommends himself to this good Mother, since her Son, as God, has promised her that for Her love He will show as much mercy as she pleases to all who recommend themselves to her? This Our Lord revealed to St. Gertrude, allowing her to hear Him make the promise to His Mother in the following words: "In My omnipotence, O revered Mother, I have granted thee the reconciliation of all sinners who devoutly invoke the aid of thy compassion, in whatever way it may please thee." ‡

On this assurance the Abbot Adam Persenius, considering the great power of Mary with God, and, at the same time, her great compassion for us, full of confidence, says: "O Mother of mercy, thy tender compassion is as great as thy power, and thou art as compassionate in forgiving as thou art powerful in obtaining all." "And when," he asks, "did the case ever occur in which thou, who art the Mother of mercy, didst not show compassion? Oh, when was it that thou, who art the Mother of omnipotence, couldst not aid? Ah, yes, with the same facility with which thou seest our misfortunes thou obtainest for us whatever thou willest." §

* *Insin.* l. 4, c. 53.　　†*Sinisc. Il Mart. di. M. ott.*
‡ *Insin.* l. 4, c. 53.　　§ *Marial.* s. 1.

"Satiate, O satiate thyself, great Queen," says the Abbot Guerric, "with the glory of thy Son, and out of compassion, though not for any merit of ours, be pleased to send us, thy servants and children here below, the crumbs that fall from thy table." *

Should the sight of our sins ever discourage us, let us address the Mother of mercy in the words of William of Paris : "O Lady, do not set up my sins against me, for I oppose thy compassion to them. Let it never be said that my sins could contend in judgment against thy mercy, which is far more powerful to obtain me pardon than my sins are to obtain my condemnation." †

Prayer.

O greatest and most sublime of all creatures, mo t sacred Virgin, I salute thee from this earth—I, a miserable and unfortunate rebel against my God, who deserve chastisements not favors, justice and not mercy. O Lady, I say not this because I doubt thy compassion. I know that the greater thou art the more thou dost glory in being benign. I know that thou rejoicest that thou art so rich, because thou art thus enabled to succor us poor miserable creatures. I know that the greater is the poverty of those who have recourse to thee, the more dost thou exert thyself to protect and save them. O my Mother, it was thou who didst one day weep over thy Son who died for me. Offer, I beseech thee, thy tears to God, and by these obtain for me true sorrow for my sins. Sinners then afflicted thee so much, and I, by my crimes, have done the same. Obtain for me, O Mary, that at least from this day forward I may not continue to afflict thee and thy Son by my ingratitude. What would thy sorrow avail me if I continued to be ungrateful to thee ? To what purpose

* *De Assumpt.* s. 4.   † *De Rhet. Div.* c. 18.

would thy mercy have been shown me, if again I was un-faithful and lost? No, my Queen, permit it not; thou hast supplied for all my shortcomings. Thou obtainest from God what thou wilt. Thou grantest the prayers of all. I ask of thee two graces: I expect them from thee, and will not be satisfied with less. Obtain for me that I may be faithful to God, and no more offend Him, and love Him during the remainder of my life as much as I have offended Him.

CHAPTER VIII.

*Et Jesum, benedictum Fructum ventris tui nobis post hoc
exilium ostende.*

AND AFTER THIS OUR EXILE SHOW UNTO US THE
BLESSED FRUIT OF THY WOMB, JESUS.

MARY, OUR SALVATION.

I. Mary delivers her Clients from Hell.

IT is impossible for a client of Mary who is faithful
in honoring and recommending himself to her to be
lost.   To some this proposition may appear at first
sight exaggerated ; but any one to whom this might
seem to be the case I would beg to suspend his judgment, and, first of all, read what I have to say on this
subject.

When we say that it is impossible for a client of
Mary to be lost, we must not be understood as speaking of those clients who take advantage of this devotion that they may sin more freely.   And therefore
those who disapprove of the great praises bestowed on
the clemency of the most blessed Virgin, because it
causes the wicked to take advantage of it to sin with
greater freedom, do so without foundation, for such
presumptive people deserve chastisement, and not
mercy, for their rash confidence.   It is therefore to be
understood of those clients who, with a sincere desire
to amend, are faithful in honoring and recommending

themselves to the Mother of God. It is, I say, morally impossible that such as these should be lost. And I find that Father Crasset,* in his book on devotion towards the Blessed Virgin Mary, says the same thing. As did also Vega, before him, in his Marian Theology, Mendoza, and other theologians. And that we may see that they did not speak at random, let us examine what other saints and learned men have said on this subject ; and let no one be surprised if many of these quotations are alike, for I have wished to give them all, in order to show how unanimous the various writers have been on the subject.

St. Anselm says, "that as it is impossible for one who is not devout to Mary, and consequently not protected by her, to be saved, so is it impossible for one who recommends himself to her, and consequently is beloved by her, to be lost."† St. Antoninus repeats the same thing and almost in the same words : "As it is impossible for those from whom Mary turns her eyes of mercy to be saved, so also are those towards whom she turns these eyes, and for whom she prays, necessarily saved and glorified." ‡ Consequently the clients of Mary will necessarily be saved.

Let us pay particular attention to the first part of the opinions of these saints, and let those tremble who make but little account of their devotion to this divine Mother, or from carelessness give it up. They say that the salvation of those who are not protected by Mary is impossible. Many others declare the same thing : such as Blessed Albert, who says, that "all those who are not thy servants, O Mary, will perish." § And St. Bonaventure : "He who neglects the service

* *Vér. Dév.* p. 1, t. 1, q. 7.   † *Orat.* 51.
‡ P. 4, tit. 15, c. 14, § 7.   § *Bibl. Mar. Is. n.* 20.

of the Blessed Virgin will die in his sins. ' Again,
" He who does not invoke thee, O Lady, will never
get to heaven." And, on the 99th Psalm the saint
even says, "that not only those from whom Mary
turns her face will not be saved, but that there will
be no hope of their salvation." * Before him, St.
Ignatius the martyr said, " that it was impossible for
any sinner to be saved without the help and favor of
the most blessed Virgin ; because those who are not
saved by the justice of God are with infinite mercy
saved by the intercession of Mary." † Some doubt
as to whether this passage is truly of St. Ignatius :
but, at all events, as Father Crasset remarks, it was
adopted by St. John Chrysostom. It is also repeated
by the Abbot of Celles. ‡ And in the same sense does
the Church apply to Mary the words of Proverbs:
" All that hate me, love death," § that is, all who do
not love me, love eternal death. For as Richard of
St. Laurence says on the words of the same book,
" She is like the merchant's ship," ‖ " All those who
are out of this ship will be lost in the sea of the
world." ¶ Even the heretical Œcolampadius looked
upon little devotion to the Mother of God as a certain
mark of reprobation. And therefore he said : " Far be
it from me ever to turn from Mary." **

But, on the other hand, Mary says in the words applied to her by the Church, " He that harkeneth to
me shall not be confounded ; " †† that is to say, he
that listeneth to what I say shall not be lost. On

* *Psalt. B. V. ps.* 116, 86, 99.
† *Ap. Lyr. Tris. Mar.* l. ii. m. 45.
‡ *Cont. de V. M. in prol.*   § Prov. viii. 36.
‖ Prov. xxxi. 14.   ¶ *De Laud. V.* l. 11.
** *S. de Laud. D. in M.*   †† Ecclus. xxiv. 30.

which St. Bonaventure says, " O Lady, he who honors
thee will be far from damnation." * And this will
still be the case, St. Hilary observes, even should the
person during the past time have greatly offended
God. " However great a sinner he may have been,"
says the saint, " if he shows himself devout to Mary,
he will never perish."

For this reason the devil does his utmost with sinners in order that, after they have lost the grace of
God, they may also lose devotion to Mary. When
Sara saw Isaac in company with Ismael, who was
teaching him evil habits, she desired that Abraham
would drive away both Ismael and his mother Agar:
" Cast out this bond-woman and her son." † She was
not satisfied with the son being turned out of the
house but insisted on the mother going also, thinking
that otherwise the son, coming to see his mother,
would continue to frequent the house. The devil,
also, is not satisfied with a soul turning out Jesus
Christ, unless it also turns out His Mother. " Cast
out this bond-woman and her Son." Otherwise He
fears that the Mother will again, by her intercession,
bring back her Son. " And his fears are well
grounded," says the learned Paciucchelli ; " for he
who is faithful in serving the Mother of God will
soon receive God Himself by the means of Mary." ‡

St. Ephrem, then, was right in calling devotion to
our blessed Lady " a charter of liberty," § our safe-
guard from hell. The same saint also calls the divine
Mother " the only hope of those who are in despair."
That which St. Bernard says is certainly true, " that
neither the power nor the will to save us can be want-

* *Psalt. B. V. ps.* 118.   † Gen. xxi. 10.
‡ *In Salv. Reg. exc.* 5.   § *Or. de Laud. V.*

ing to Mary;"* the power cannot be wanting, for it is impossible that her prayers should not be heard; as St. Antoninus says, "It is impossible that a Mother of God should pray in vain;"† and St. Bernard says the same thing, "that her requests can never be refused, but that she obtains whatever she wills."‡ The will to save us cannot be wanting, for Mary is our Mother, and desires our salvation more than we can desire it ourselves. Since, then, this is the case, how can it be possible for a client of Mary to be lost? He may be a sinner, but if he recommends himself to this good Mother with perseverance and purpose of amendment, she will undertake to obtain him light to abandon his wicked state, sorrow for his sins, perseverance in virtue, and finally a good death. And what mother would not deliver her son from death if it only depended on her asking the favor to obtain it from the judge? And can we think that Mary, who loves her clients with a mother's most tender love, will not deliver her child from eternal death when she can do it so easily?

Ah, devout reader, let us thank Our Lord if we see that He has given us affection for the Queen of heaven, and confidence in her; "for," says St. John Damascene, "God only grants this favor to those whom He is determined to save." The following are the beautiful words of the saint, and with which he rekindles his own and our hope: "O Mother of God, if I place my confidence in thee, I shall be saved. If I am under thy protection, I have nothing to fear, for the fact of being thy client is the possession of a certainty of salvation, which God

---

In Assumpt. s. 1.   † P. 4, tit. 15, c. 17.   ‡ *De Aquæd.*

only grants to those whom He intends to save." *
Therefore, Erasmus salutes the Blessed Virgin in
these words : " Hail ! O terror of hell; O hope of
Christians; confidence in thee is a pledge of salvation." †

Oh, how enraged is the devil when he sees a soul
persevering in devotion to the divine Mother! We
read in the Life of Blessed Alphonsus Rodriguez,
who was very devout to Mary, that once when in
prayer, finding himself much troubled by the devil
with impure thoughts, this enemy said : " Give up thy
devotion to Mary, and I will cease to tempt thee."

We read in Blosius that God revealed to St. Catha-
rine of Siena, " that in His goodness, and on account
of the Incarnate Word, He had granted to Mary, who
was His Mother, that no one, not even a sinner, who
devoutly recommends himself to her should ever become the prey of hell." ‡ Even the Prophet David
prayed to be delivered from hell, for the sake of the
love he bore to Mary. " I have loved, O Lord, the
beauty of Thy house . . . take not away my soul,
O God, with the wicked." § He says " of Thy house,"
for Mary was the house that God himself constructed
for His dwelling on earth, and in which He could find
repose on becoming man, as it is written in the Book
of Proverbs : " Wisdom hath built herself a house." ‖
" No," says St. Ignatius the martyr ; " he who is devout to the Virgin Mother will certainly never be
lost." ¶ And St. Bonaventure confirms this, saying,
" Thy lovers, O Lady, enjoy peace in this life, and
will never see eternal death." ** The devout Blosius

* *Crasset, Vér. Dév.* p. 1, tr. 1, q. 6.　　† *Pœan ad Virg.*
‡ *Conc. an. fid.* p. 2, c. i.　§ Ps. xxv. 8.　‖ Prov. ix. 1.
¶ *Lohner, Bibl.* t. 70, § 3.　　** *Psalt. B. V. ps.* 67.

assures us, "that the case never did and never will occur in which a humble and attentive servant of Mary was lost." *

"Oh, how many would have remained obstinate in sin, and have been eternally lost," says Thomas à Kempis, "if Mary had not interposed with her Son that He might show them mercy!" † It is also the opinion of many theologians, and of St. Thomas ‡ in particular, that for many who have died in mortal sin the divine Mother has obtained from God a suspension of their sentence and a return to life to do penance.

Trustworthy authors give us many instances in which this has occurred.§ Amongst others, Flodoardus, who lived about the ninth century, relates in his Chronicles, ‖ that a certain deacon named Adelman, who was apparently dead, and was being buried, returned to life, and said "that he had seen hell, to which he was condemned, but that, at the prayers of

---

* *Par. an. fid.* p. 1, c. 18.

† *Ad Nov.* s. 23.   ‡ *Suppl.* q. 71, a. 5.

§ In view of these examples and of those that we read farther on, there arises the twofold question, *De jure et de facto.* Question *de jure :* Can God hinder, and can the Blessed Virgin obtain by her prayers, that condemnation to hell be not put in execution ? With these theologians, and notably with St. Alphonsus, there is no one who could not answer, Yes. Question *de facto*: Has it happened, thanks to the prayers of the Blessed Virgin, that sinners condemned to hell have not been plunged into it, and that by a good confession they have effaced the sentence of their condemnation ? Yes ; for the facts that I cite, says St. Alphonsus, are affirmed by trustworthy authors as real and public facts.—ED.

‖ *Chron. eccl. Rem. anno* 934.

the Blessed Virgin, he had been sent back to this
world to do penance."

Surius relates a similar case * of a Roman citizen
named Andrew, who had died impenitent, and for
whom Mary obtained that he should come to life
again, that he might be pardoned. Pelbertus † says,
"that in his time, when the Emperor Sigismund was
crossing the Alps with his army, a voice was heard
coming from a skeleton, asking for a confessor, and
declaring that the Mother of God, for whom he had had
a tender devotion when a soldier, had obtained that
he should thus live until he had been able to make
his confession ; and, having done so, the soul departed." ‡

These, and other such examples, however, must not
encourage rash persons to live in sin, with the hope
that Mary will deliver them from hell even should
they die in this state ; for as it would be the height
of folly for any one to throw himself into a well with

* 4 *Dec. S. Ann.* l. 1, c. 35.

† *Stellar*, *B. V.* l. 12, p. 2, a. 1.

‡ This is undoubtedly a very strange fact. However,
who will dispute it, either by limiting the power of God or
the influence of the Blessed Virgin, or by refusing to believe the authority of a writer such as Father Pelbart, who,
in a book dedicated to Pope Sixtus IV., relates in detail
this prodigy as having happened at this time in the presence of an illustrious emperor and the members of his
court, several of whom, as they were yet living, could have
convicted him of falsehood, if he had not told the truth?
This reflection is made by Father Crasset ; it may also be
applied to other examples not less wonderful. Moreover,
the miracle of which there is question here is affirmed by a
great number of most respectable authors; among them
Lyræus is distinguished by his most circumstantial narra-
tive in his *Trisagion Marianum*, l. 1, son. 31.—ED.

a hope that Mary would preserve his life because she has occasionally preserved some under similar circumstances, still greater folly would it be to run the risk of dying in sin, in the hope that the Blessed Virgin would save him from hell. But these examples serve to revive our confidence with the reflection, that if the divine Mother has been able to deliver from hell even some who have died in sin, how much more will she be able to preserve from a similar lot those who, during life, have recourse to her with a purpose of amendment, and who serve her faithfully.

"What, then, will be our lot, O tender Mother," let us ask with St. Germanus, "who are sinners, but desire to change, and have recourse to thee, who art the life of Christians?"[*]   St. Anselm says, "that he will not be lost for whom thou once prayest." Oh, pray, then, for us, and we shall be preserved from hell. "Who," exclaims Richard of St. Victor, "will presume to say, if I have thee to defend me, O Mother of mercy, that the Judge will be unfavorable to me when I am presented before the divine tribunal?"[†]   Blessed Henry Suso used to say, "that he had placed his soul in the hands of Mary, and that if he was condemned, the sentence must pass through her hands;"[‡] being confident that if it was in such hands, this tender Virgin would certainly prevent its execution. The same do I hope for myself, O my own most holy Queen; and therefore I will always repeat the words of St. Bonaventure: "In thee, O Lady, have I placed all my hopes; and thus I confidently trust that I shall never be lost, but praise and love thee forever in heaven."[§]

[*] *De Zona Virg.*   [†] *In Cant.* c. 39.
[‡] *Hor. Sap. æt.* l. 1, c. 16.   [§] *Psalt. B. V. ps.* 30.

Prayer.

O Mary, my most dear Mother, in what an abyss of evils should I not now be, if thou hadst not so many times delivered me with thy compassionate hand! How many years ago should I not have been in hell, hadst thou not saved me by thy powerful prayers! My grievous sins already drove me there; divine justice had already condemned me; the devils already longed to execute the sentence; and thou didst fly to my aid, and save me without being even called or asked. And what return can I make to thee, O my beloved protectress, for so many favors and for such love? Thou also didst overcome the hardness of my heart, and didst draw me to thy love and to confidence in thee. And into how many other evils should I not have fallen, if with thy compassionate hand thou hadst not so often helped me in the dangers into which I was on the point of falling! Continue, O my hope, to preserve me from hell, and from the sins into which I may still fall. Never allow me to have this misfortune—to curse thee in hell. My beloved Lady, I love thee. Can thy goodness ever endure to see a servant of thine that loves thee lost? Ah! then, obtain that I may nevermore be ungrateful to thee and to my God, who for the love of thee has granted me so many graces. O Mary, tell me, shall I be lost? Yes, if I abandon thee. But is this possible? Can I ever forget the love thou hast borne me? Thou, after God, art the love of my soul. I can no longer trust myself to live without loving thee. O most beautiful, most holy, most amiable, sweetest creature in the world, I rejoice in thy happiness, I love thee, and I hope always to love thee both in time and in eternity. Amen.

II. Mary succors her Clients in Purgatory.

Fortunate, indeed, are the clients of this most compassionate Mother; for not only does she succor them in this world, but even in purgatory they are helped and comforted by her protection. And as in that prison poor souls are in the greatest need of assistance, since in their torments they cannot help themselves, our Mother of mercy does proportionately more to relieve them. St. Bernardine of Siena says, "that in that prison, where souls that are spouses of Jesus Christ are detained, Mary has a certain dominion and plenitude of power, not only to relieve them, but even to deliver them from their pains." *

And, first, with respect to the relief she gives. The same saint in applying those words of Ecclesiasticus, "I have walked in the waves of the sea," † adds, "that it is by visiting and relieving the necessities and torments of her clients, who are her children." He then says "that the pains of purgatory are called waves, because they are transitory, unlike the pains of hell, which never end ; and they are called waves of the sea, because they are so bitter. The clients of Mary, thus suffering, are often visited and relieved by her." " See, therefore," says Novarinus, "of what consequence it is to be the servant of this good Lady, for her servants she never forgets when they are suffering in those flames ; for though Mary relieves all suffering souls in purgatory, yet she always obtains far greater indulgence and relief for her own clients." ‡

The divine Mother once addressed these words to St. Bridget: "I am the Mother of all souls in purgatory ; for all the pains that they have deserved for their sins are every hour, as long as they remain there, in some way mitigated by my prayers." § The compassionate Mother even condescends to go herself occasionally into that holy prison, to visit and comfort

* *Pro Fest. V. M.* s. 3, a. 2, c. 3.   † Ecclus. xxiv. 8.
‡ *Umbra Virg. exc.* 86.   § Rev. l. 4, c. 138.

her suffering children. St. Bonaventure, applying to
Mary the words of Ecclesiasticus, " I have penetrated
into the bottom of the deep," * says, " the deep, that
is, purgatory, to relieve by my presence the holy souls
detained there." " Oh, how courteous and benign is
the most blessed Virgin," says St. Vincent Ferrer, " to
those who suffer in purgatory ! through her they constantly receive comfort and refreshment." †

And what other consolation have they in their sufferings than Mary, and the relief they receive from this
Mother of mercy ? St. Bridget once heard Jesus say
to His holy Mother, " thou art My Mother, the
Mother of mercy, and the consolation of souls in
purgatory." The Blessed Virgin herself told the
saint, " that as a poor sick person, bedridden, suffering, and abandoned, is relieved by words of encour-
agement and consolation, so are the souls in purgatory
consoled and relieved by only hearing her name." ‡
The mere name of Mary, that name of hope and salvation, which is frequently invoked by her beloved
children in their prison, is a great source of comfort to them ; "for," says Novarinus, " that loving
Mother no sooner hears them call upon her than she
offers her prayers to God, and these prayers, as a heavenly dew, immediately refresh them in their burning
pains." §

Mary not only consoles and relieves her clients in
purgatory, but she delivers them by her prayers. Gerson says, " that on the day of her assumption into
heaven purgatory was entirely emptied." ‖ Novarinus
confirms this, saying, " that it is maintained by many

* Ecclus. xxiv. 8.   † *In Nat. B. V.* s. 2.
‡ Rev. l. i, c. 16, 9.   § *Umbra Virg. exc.* 86.
‖ *Super Magn.* tr. 4.

grave authors, that when Mary was going to heaven, she asked as a favor from her Son to take all the souls then in purgatory with her." *   "And from that time forward," says Gerson, " Mary had the privilege of delivering her servants." †   St. Bernardine of Siena also positively asserts "that the Blessed Virgin has the power of delivering souls from purgatory, but particularly those of her clients, by her prayers, and by applying her merits for them."   Novarinus says, " that by the merits of Mary, not only are the pains of those souls lessened, but the time of their sufferings is shortened through her intercession." ‡   She has only to ask, and all is done.

St. Peter Damian relates, " that a lady named Marozia appeared after her death to her godmother, and told her that on the feast of the Assumption she, together with a multitude exceeding the population of Rome, had been delivered by Mary from purgatory." §   Denis the Carthusian says, " that on the feasts of the Nativity and Resurrection of Jesus Christ Mary does the same thing ; for on those days, accompanied by choirs of angels, she visits that prison and delivers very many souls from their torments." ‖   Novarinus says, " that he can easily believe that on all her own solemn feasts she delivers many souls from their sufferings." ¶

The promise made by our blessed Lady to Pope John XXII. is well known. She appeared to him, and ordered him to make known to all that on the Saturday after their death she would deliver from purgatory all who wore the Carmelite scapular. This, as

* *Loco supra cit.*   † *Pro Fest. V. M.* s. 3, a. 2, c. 3.
‡ *Loco cit.*   § *Opusc.* 34, c. 3.
‖ *In Assumpt.* s. 2.   ¶ *Loco cit.*

Father Crasset* relates, was proclaimed by the same Pontiff in a Bull, which was afterwards confirmed by Alexander V., Clement VII., Pius V., Gregory XIII., and Paul V.; and this latter, in a Bull of the year 1613, says "that Christian people may piously believe that the Blessed Virgin will help them after death by her continual intercession, her merits, and special protection ; and that on Saturdays, the day consecrated by the Church to her, she will in a more particular manner help the souls of the brethren of the Confraternity of Our Blessed Lady of Mount Carmel who have departed this life in a state of grace, provided they have worn the habit, observed the chastity of their state, and recited her office : or, if they could not recite it, if they have observed the fasts of the Church, and abstained from meat on all Wednesdays except Christmas-day." In the solemn office of our blessed Lady of Mount Carmel we read that it is piously believed that the Blessed Virgin comforts the brethren of this confraternity in purgatory with maternal love, and that by her intercession she soon delivers them, and takes them to heaven.†

Why should we not hope for the same graces and favors, if we are devout clients of this good Mother ? And if we serve her with more special love, why can we not hope to go to heaven immediately after death, without even going to purgatory ? This really took place in the case of Blessed Godfrey, to whom Mary sent the following message, by Brother Abondo : " Tell Brother Godfrey to endeavor to advance rapidly in virtue, and thus he will belong to my Son and to me : and when his soul departs, I will not allow it to go

---

* *Vér. Dév.* p. 2, tr. 6, pr. 4.   † *Die* 16 *jul. lect.* 6.

to purgatory, but will take it and offer it to my Son." *

Finally, if we wish to relieve the holy souls in purgatory, let us do so by imploring the aid of our blessed Lady in all our prayers, and especially by offering the Rosary for them, as that relieves them greatly.

Prayer

O Queen of heaven and earth! O Mother of the Lord of the world! O Mary, of all creatures the greatest, the most exalted, and the most amiable! it is true that there are many in this world who neither know thee nor love thee; but in heaven there are many millions of angels and blessed spirits, who love and praise thee continually. Even in the world, how many happy souls are there not who burn with thy love, and live enamoured of thy goodness! Oh, that I also could love thee, O Lady worthy of all love! Oh, that I could always remember to serve thee, to praise thee, to honor thee, and engage all to love thee! Thou hast attracted the love of God, whom, by thy beauty, thou hast, so to say, torn from the bosom of His Eternal Father, and engaged to become man, and be thy Son. And shall I, a poor worm of the earth, not be enamoured of thee? No, my most sweet Mother, I also will love thee much, and will do all that I can to make others love thee also. Accept, then, O Mary, the desire that I have to love thee, and help me to execute it. I know how favorably thy lovers are looked upon by God. He, after his own glory, desires nothing more than thine, and to see thee honored and loved by all. From thee, O Lady, do I expect all; through thee the remission of my sins, through thee perseverance. Thou must assist me at death, and deliver me from purgatory; and finally, thou must lead me to heaven. All this thy lovers hope

* *Men. Cist. 2 Oct.*

from thee, and are not deceived. I, who love thee with so much affection and above all other things after God, hope for the same favors.

III. Mary leads her Servants to Heaven.

Oh, what an evident mark of predestination have the servants of Mary! The holy Church, for the consolation of her clients, puts into her mouth the words of Ecclesiasticus, "In all these I sought rest, and I shall abide in the inheritance of the Lord." * Cardinal Hugo explains these words, and says, "blessed is he in whose house the most holy Virgin finds repose." Mary, out of the love she bears to all, endeavors to excite in all devotion towards herself; many either do not admit it into their souls, or do not preserve it. But blessed is he that receives and preserves it. "And I shall abide in the inheritance of the Lord." "That is," adds the Cardinal, "Blessed is he whose interior offers the Blessed Virgin Mary a place of repose." Devotion towards the Blessed Virgin remains in all who are the inheritance of Our Lord; that is to say, in all who will praise Him eternally in heaven. Mary continues, speaking in the words of Ecclesiasticus : "He that made me rested in my tabernacle, and He said to me : Let thy dwelling be in Jacob, and thy inheritance in Israel ; and take root in My elect." That is, my Creator has condescended to come and repose in my bosom, and His will is, that I should dwell in the hearts of all the elect (of whom Jacob was a figure, and who are the inheritance of the Blessed Virgin), and that devotion and confidence in me should take root in all the predestined.

* Ecclus. xxiv. 11.

Oh, how many blessed souls are there now in heaven who would never have been there had not Mary, by her powerful intercession, led them thither: "I made that in the heavens there should rise light that never faileth." * Cardinal Hugo, in his commentary on the above text of Ecclesiasticus, says, in the name of Mary, "I have caused as many lights to shine eternally in heaven as I have clients"; and then he adds, "There are many saints in heaven through her intercession, who would never have been there but through her."

St. Bonaventure says, "that the gates of heaven will open to all who confide in the protection of Mary." † Hence, St. Ephrem calls devotion to the divine Mother "the unlocking of the gates of the heavenly Jerusalem." ‡ The devout Blosius also, addressing our blessed Lady, says, "To thee, O Lady, are committed the keys and the treasures of the kingdom of heaven." § And therefore we ought constantly to pray to her, in the words of St. Ambrose, "Open to us, O Mary, the gates of paradise, since thou hast its keys." Nay more, the Church says, that "thou art its gate."

For the same reason, again, is this great Mother called by the Church the Star of the Sea. "Hail, Star of the Sea!" "For," says the angelical St. Thomas, "as sailors are guided by a star to the port, so are Christians guided to heaven by Mary." ‖

For the same reason, finally, is she called by St. Fulgentius, "the heavenly ladder." "For," says the saint, "by Mary God descended from heaven into the world, that by her men might ascend from earth to

* Ecclus. xxiv. 6.   † *Psalt. B. V. ps.* 90.

‡ *De Laud. Dei gen.*   § *Par. anfid.* p. 2, c. 4.

‖ *Exp. in Sal. Ang.*

heaven."* "And thou, O Lady," says St. Athanasius, "wast filled with grace, that thou mightest be the way of our salvation, and the means of ascent to the heavenly kingdom."†

St. Bernard calls our blessed Lady "the heavenly chariot." ‡ And St. John Geometra salutes her, saying, "Hail, resplendent car!"§ signifying that she is the car in which her clients mount to heaven. "Blessed are they who know thee, O Mother of God," says St. Bonaventure; "for the knowledge of thee is the high road to everlasting life, and the publication of thy virtues is the way of eternal salvation." ‖

In the Franciscan chronicles it is related that Brother Leo once saw a red ladder, on the summit of which was Jesus Christ; and a white one, on the top of which was His most holy Mother; and he saw some who tried to ascend the red ladder, and they mounted a few steps and fell—they tried again, and again fell. They were then advised to go and try the white ladder, and by that one they easily ascended, for our blessed Lady stretched out her hand and helped them, and so they got safely to heaven.¶

Denis the Carthusian asks: "Who is there that is saved? who is there that reigns in heaven?" And he answers, "They are certainly saved and reign in heaven for whom this Queen of mercy intercedes." ** And this Mary herself confirms in the Book of Proverbs: "By me kings reign;" †† through my intercession souls reign, first in this mortal life by ruling their passions, and so come to reign eternally in heaven,

* *In Annunt,* s. 1.   † *In Annunt.* s. 1.
‡ *De Aquæd.*   § *In V. Deip.* h. 1.
‖ *Psalt. B. V. ps.* 85.   ¶ *Wadding, Ann.* 1232, n. 28.
** *Paciucch. Sup. Salve Reg. exc.* 1.   †† Prov. viii. 15.

where, says St. Augustine, "all are kings." "Mary, in fine," says Richard of St. Laurence, "is the mistress of heaven ; for there she commands as she wills, and admits whom she wills." And applying to her the words of Ecclesiasticus, "And my power was in Jerusalem," * he makes her say, "I command what I will, and introduce whom I will." † Our blessed Lady being Mother of the Lord of heaven, it is reasonable that she also should be sovereign Lady of that kingdom, according to Rupert, who says, "that by right she possesses the whole kingdom of her Son." ‡

St. Antoninus tells us "that this divine Mother has already, by her assistance and prayers, obtained heaven for us, provided we put no obstacle in the way." § Hence, says the Abbot Guerric, "he who serves Mary, and for whom she intercedes, is as certain of heaven as if he was already there." St. John Damascene also says, "that to serve Mary and be her courtier is the greatest honor we can possibly possess ; for to serve the Queen of heaven is already to reign there, and to live under her commands is more than to govern." On the other hand, he adds, "that those who do not serve Mary will not be saved ; for those who are deprived of the help of this great Mother are also deprived of that her Son and of the whole court of heaven." ‖

"May the infinite goodness of Our Lord be ever praised," says St. Bernard, for having been pleased to give us Mary as our advocate in heaven, that she, being at the same time the Mother of our Judge and a Mother of mercy, may be able, by her intercession,

* Ecclus. xxiv. 15.   † De Laud. Virg. l. 4, c. 4.
‡ In Cant. l. 3.   § Paciucch. Sup. Salve Reg. exc. 1.
‖ De Laud. B. M. l. 4.

to conduct to a prosperous issue the great affair of
our eternal salvation."* St. James, a Doctor of the
Greek Church, says, "that God destined Mary as a
bridge of salvation, by using which we might with
safety pass over the stormy sea of this world, and
reach the happy haven of paradise." † Therefore St.
Bonaventure exclaims, "Give ear, O ye nations; and
all you who desire heaven, serve, honor Mary, and
certainly you will find eternal life." ‡

Nor should those even who have deserved hell be
in the least doubtful as to obtaining heaven, provided
they are faithful in serving this Queen. "Oh, how
many sinners," says St. Germanus, "have found God
and have been saved by thy means, O Mary!" §
Richard of St. Laurence remarks, that St. John in the
Apocalypse says that Mary was crowned with stars:
"and on her head a crown of twelve stars." ‖ On
the other hand, in the sacred Canticles, she is said to
be crowned with wild beasts, lions, and leopards:
"Come from Libanus, my spouse, come from Libanus,
come; thou shalt be crowned . . . from the dens of
the lions, from the mountains of the leopards." ¶
How is this? He answers, that "these wild beasts
are sinners, who by the favor and intercession of Mary
have become stars of paradise, better adapted to the
head of this Queen of mercy than all the material
stars of heaven." **

We read in the life of the servant of God, Sister
Seraphina of Capri, that once during the novena of
the Assumption of Mary she asked our blessed Lady
for the conversion of a thousand sinners, but after-

* *In Assumpt.* s. 1.　　† *Or. in Nat. Dei gen.*
‡ *Psalt. B. V. ps.* 48.　　§ *In Dorm. V. M.* s. 2.
‖ Apoc. xii. 1.　¶ Cant. iv. 8.　** *De Laud. B. M.* l. 3.

wards thought that she had asked too much; and
then the Blessed Virgin appeared to her, and corrected
her for her ungrounded anxiety, saying, " Why dost
thou fear ?   Is it that I am not sufficiently powerful
to obtain from my Son the conversion of a thousand
sinners ?   See, I have already obtained the favor."
With these words she took her in spirit to heaven,
and there showed her innumerable souls that had
deserved hell, but had been saved through her intercession, and were already enjoying eternal happiness.

It is true that in this world no one can be certain
of his salvation : " Man knoweth not whether he be
worthy of love or hatred," says Ecclesiastes.*   But
St. Bonaventure, on the words of King David, " Lord,
who shall dwell in Thy tabernacle ?" † and on the
preceding quotation, answers, " Sinners, let us follow
Mary closely, and casting ourselves at her feet, let us
not leave them until she has blessed us ; for her blessing will insure our salvation." ‡

" It suffices, O Lady, " says St. Anselm, " that thou
willest it, and our salvation is certain." §   And St. Antoninus says that " souls protected by Mary, and on
which she casts her eyes, are necessarily justified and
saved." ‖

" With reason, therefore," observes St. Ildephonsus,
" did the most holy Virgin predict that all generations
would call her blessed ;" " for all the elect obtain
eternal salvation through the means of Mary." ¶   " And
thou, O great Mother," says St. Methodius, " art the
beginning, the middle, and the end of our happiness;"**
—the beginning, for Mary obtains us the pardon of

---

* Eccles. ix. 1.   † Ps. xiv. 1.   ‡ *Psalt. B. V. ps.* 14.
§ *De Excell. Virg.* c. 6.   ‖ P. 4, tit. 15, c. 17, § 7.
¶ *De Assumpt.* s. 3.   ** *De Sim. et Anna.*

our sins; the middle, for she obtains us perseverance in divine grace ; and the end, for she finally obtains us heaven. " By thee, O Mary, was heaven opened," says St. Bernard ; " by thee was hell emptied ; by thee was paradise restored; and through thee, in fine, is eternal life given to so many miserable creatures who deserved eternal death." *

But that which above all should encourage us to hope with confidence for heaven, is the beautiful promise made by Mary herself to all who honor her, and especially to those who, by word and example, endeavor to make her known and honored by others: " They that work by me shall not sin ; they that explain me shall have life everlasting." † " Oh, happy they who obtain the favor of Mary ! " exclaims St. Bonaventure ; " they will be recognized by the blessed as their companions, and whoever bears the stamp of a servant of Mary is already enrolled in the Book of Life." ‡

Why, then, should we trouble ourselves about the opinions of scholastics as to whether predestination to glory precedes or follows the prevision of merits? If we are true servants of Mary, and obtain her protection, we most certainly shall be inscribed in the Book of Life ; for, says St. John Damascene, " God only grants devotion towards His most holy Mother to those whom He will save." This is also clearly expressed by Our Lord in St. John : " He that shall overcome . . . I will write upon him the name of My God, and the name of the city of My God." § And who but Mary is this city of God ? observes St. Gregory on the

words of St. David : " Glorious things are said of thee,
O city of God." *

Correctly, then, can we here say with St. Paul,
" Having this seal, the Lord knoweth who are His ;" †
that is to say, whoever carries with him the mark of
devotion to Mary is recognized by God as His. Hence
St. Bernard writes, "that devotion to the Mother of God
is a most certain mark of eternal salvation." ‡ Blessed
Alan, speaking of the Hail Mary, also says, that
" whoever often honors our blessed Lady with this angelical salutation has a very great mark of predestination." He says the same thing of perseverance in
the daily recital of the Rosary, "that those who do
so have a very great assurance of salvation." § Father
Nieremberg says, in the tenth chapter of his book on
" Affection for Mary," that " the servants of the
Mother of God are not only privileged and favored in
this world, but even in heaven they are more particularly honored." He then adds : " that in heaven they
will be recognized as servants of its Queen, and as be-
longing to her court, by a distinguishing and richer
garment," according to the words of the Proverbs, " All
her domestics are clothed with double garments." ‖

St. Mary Magdalen of Pazzi saw a vessel in the
midst of the sea : in it were all the clients of Mary,
and the Blessed Mother herself steered it safely into
port. By this the saint understood that those who live
under the protection of Mary are secure, in the midst
of the dangers of this life, from the shipwreck of sin,
and from eternal damnation ; for she guides them
safely into the haven of salvation. Let us then enter

* Ps. lxxxvi. 3.   † 2 Tim. ii. 19.
‡ *Stell. B. V.* l. 12, p. 2, a. 1.
§ *De Psalt.* p. 2, c. 11.—p. 4, c. 24.   ‖ Prov. xxxi. 21.

this blessed ship of the mantle of Mary, and there we can be certain of the kingdom of heaven; for the Church says: "O holy Mother of God, all those who will be partakers of eternal happiness dwell in thee, living under thy protection." *

Prayer.

O Queen of heaven, Mother of holy love! since thou art the most amiable of creatures, the most beloved of God, and His greatest lover, be pleased to allow the most miserable sinner living in this world, who, having by thy means been delivered from hell, and without any merit on his part been so benefited by thee and who is filled with love for thee, to love thee. I would desire, were it in my power, to let all men who know thee not know how worthy thou art of love, that all might love and honor thee. I would desire to die for the love of thee, in defence of thy virginity, of thy dignity of Mother of God, of thy Immaculate Conception, should this be necessary, to uphold these thy great privileges. Ah! my most beloved Mother, accept this my ardent desire, and never allow a servant of thine, who loves thee, to become the enemy of thy God, whom thou lovest so much. Alas! poor me, I was so for a time, when I offended my Lord. But then, O Mary, I loved thee but little, and strove but little to be beloved by thee. But now there is nothing that I so much desire, after the grace of God, as to love and be loved by thee. I am not discouraged on account of my past sins, for I know that thou, O most benign and gracious Lady, dost not disdain to love even the most wretched sinners who love thee; nay more, that thou never allowest thyself to be surpassed by any in love. Ah! Queen most worthy of love, I desire to love thee in heaven. There, at thy feet, I shall better know how worthy thou art of love, how much thou hast done to save

* *Off. ad Mat.*

me; and thus I shall love thee with greater love, and love thee eternally, without fear of ever ceasing to love thee. O Mary, I hope most certainly to be saved by thy means. Pray to Jesus for me.   Nothing else is needed ; thou hast to save me ; thou art my hope.   I will therefore always sing, O Mary, my hope, thou hast to save me !

CHAPTER IX.

O Clemens, O Pia !

O MERCIFUL, O PIOUS.

CLEMENCY AND COMPASSION OF MARY.

How great are the Clemency and Compassion of Mary.

ST. BERNARD, speaking of the great compassion of
Mary towards us poor creatures, says, "that she is the
land overflowing with milk and honey promised by
God."* Hence St. Leo observes, "that the Blessed
Virgin has so merciful a heart, that she deserves not
only to be called merciful, but mercy itself." St.
Bonaventure also, considering that Mary was made
Mother of God on account of the miserable, and that
to her is committed the charge of dispensing mercy,
considering, moreover, the tender care she takes of
all, and that her compassion is so great that she seems
to have no other desire than that of relieving the
needy, says, that when he looks at her, he seems no
longer to see the justice of God, but only the divine
mercy, of which Mary is full. "O Lady, when I behold thee, I can only discern mercy, for thou wast
made Mother of God for the wretched, and then thou
wast intrusted with their charge : thou art all solicitude for them ; thou art walled in with mercy ; thy
only wish is to show it." †

* *In Salve Reg.* s. 3.   † *Stim. div. am.* p. 3, c. 19.

In fine, the compassion of Mary is so great towards us, that the Abbot Guerric says, " that her loving heart can never remain a moment without bringing forth its fruits of tenderness." * " And what," exclaims St. Bernard, " can ever flow from a source of compassion but compassion itself ? " †

Mary is also called an olive-tree : " As a fair olive-tree on the plains." ‡ For as from the olive oil (a symbol of mercy) alone is extracted, so from the hands of Mary graces and mercy alone proceed. Hence the venerable Father Louis de Ponte says, " that Mary may properly be called the Mother of oil, since she is the Mother of mercy." § And thus, when we go to this good Mother for the oil of her mercy, we cannot fear that she will deny it to us, as the wise virgins in the gospel did to the foolish ones, " lest perhaps there be not enough for us and for you." ‖ Oh, no ! for she is indeed rich in this oil of mercy, as St. Bonaventure assures us, " Mary is filled with the oil of compassion." ¶ She is called by the Church not only a prudent virgin, but most prudent, that we may understand, says Hugo of St. Victor, that she is so full of grace and compassion, that she can supply all, without losing any herself. " Thou, O Blessed Virgin, art full of grace, and indeed so full, that the whole world may draw of this overflowing oil." " For if the prudent virgins provided oil in vessels with their lamps, thou, O most prudent Virgin, hast borne an overflowing and inexhaustible vessel, from which, the oil of mercy streaming, thou replenishest the lamps of all." **

But why, I ask, is this beautiful olive-tree said to

---

* *De Assumpt.* s. 1.   † *Dom.* 1. *p. Epiph.* s. 1.
‡ Ecclus. xxiv. 19.   § *In Cant.* l. 1, *exh.* 21.
‖ Matt. xxv. 9.   ¶ *Spec. B. M.V. lect.* 7.   ** *De Verb. Inc.*c.3.

stand in the midst of the plains, and not rather in the midst of a garden, surrounded by a wall and hedges? The same Hugo of St. Victor tells us, that it is " that all may see her, that all may go to her for refuge ; " * that all may see her easily, and as easily have recourse to her, to obtain remedies for all their ills. This beautiful explanation is confirmed by St. Antoninus, who says, " that all can go to, and gather the fruit of, an olive-tree that is exposed in the midst of a plain ; and thus all, both just and sinners, can have recourse to Mary, to obtain her mercy." He then adds, " Oh, how many sentences of condemnation has not this most blessed Virgin revoked by her compassionate prayers, in favor of sinners who have had recourse to her ! " † " And what safer refuge," says the devout Thomas à Kempis, " can we ever find than the compassionate heart of Mary ? There the poor find a home, the infirm a remedy, the afflicted relief, the doubtful counsel, and the abandoned succor." ‡

Wretched indeed should we be, had we not this Mother of mercy always attentive and solicitous to relieve us in our wants ! " Where there is no woman he mourneth that is in want," § says the Holy Ghost. " This woman," says St. John Damascene, " is precisely the most blessed Virgin Mary ; and wherever this most holy woman is not the sick man groans." And surely it cannot be otherwise, since all graces are dispensed at the prayer of Mary ; and where this is wanting, there can be no hope of mercy, as Our Lord gave St. Bridget to understand in these words : " Unless the prayers of Mary interposed, there could be no hope of mercy." ‖

* *De Assumpt.* s. 2.   † P. 3, t 31, c. 4, § 3.   ‡ *Ad Nov.* s. 24.
   § Ecclus. xxxvi. 27.   ‖ Rev. l. 6, c. 26.

But perhaps we fear that Mary does not see, or does not feel for, our necessities? Oh, no, she sees and feels them far better than we do ourselves. "There is not one amongst all the saints," says St. Antoninus, "who can ever feel for us in our miseries, both corporal and spiritual, like this woman, the most blessed Virgin Mary." * So much so, that there where she sees misery, she canno do otherwise than instantly fly and relieve it with her tender compassion. † Richard of St. Victor repeats the same thing; and Mendoza says, "Therefore, O most blessed Virgin, thou dispensest thy mercies with a generous hand, wherever thou seest necessities." ‡ Our good Mother herself protests that she will never cease to fulfil this office of mercy: "And unto the world to come I shall not cease to be, and in the holy dwelling-place I have ministered before him;" § that is, as Cardinal Hugo explains, "I will never cease until the end of the world relieving the miseries of men, and praying for sinners," that they may be delivered from eternal misery, and be saved.

Suetonius relates,‖ that the Emperor Titus was so desirous of rendering service to those who applied to him, that, when a day passed without being able to grant a favor, he used to say with sorrow, "I have lost a day; for I have spent it without benefiting any one." It is probable that Titus spoke thus more from vanity and the desire of being esteemed than from true charity. But should such a thing happen to our Empress Mary, as to have to pass a day without granting a grace, she would speak as Titus did, but

* P. 4, tit. 15, c. 2.   † *In Cant.* c. 23.
‡ *In Reg.* c. iv. n. 11, *ann.* 12.   § Ecclus. xxiv. 14.
‖ *In Tit.* c. 8.

from a true desire to serve us, and because she is full of charity. "So much so, indeed," says Bernardine de Bustis, "that she is more anxious to grant us graces than we are to receive them." "And therefore," says the same author, "whenever we go to her, we always find her hands filled with mercy and liberality." *

Rebecca was a figure of Mary; and she, when asked by Abraham's servant for a little water to drink, replied, that not only would she give him plenty for himself, but also for his camels, saying, "I will draw water for thy camels also, till they all drink." † On these words St. Bernard addresses our blessed Lady, saying: "O Mary, thou art far more liberal and compassionate than Rebecca; and therefore thou art not satisfied with distributing the treasures of thy immense mercy only to the just, of whom Abraham's servants were types, but also thou bestowest them on sinners who are signified by the camels." ‡ "The liberality of Mary," says Richard of St. Laurence, "is like that of her Son, who always gives more than He is asked for." § "He is," says St. Paul, "rich unto all that call upon Him." ‖ "And the liberality of Mary is like His: she bestows more than is sought." Hear how a devout writer thus addresses the Blessed Virgin: "O Lady do thou pray for me, for thou wilt ask for the graces I require with greater devotion than I can dare to ask for them; and thou wilt obtain far greater graces from God for me than I can presume to seek." ¶

When the Samaritans refused to receive Jesus Christ and His doctrines, St. James and St. John asked Him

---

* *Marial.* p. 2, s. 5. † Gen. xxiv. 19.
‡ *In Sign. Magn.* § *De Laud. B. M.* l. 4. ‖ Rom. x. 12.
¶ *De Rhet. div.* c. 18.

whether they should command fire to fall from heaven and devour them ; Our Lord replied, " You know not of what spirit you are." *   As if He had said, " I am of so tender and compassionate a spirit that I came from heaven to save and not to chastise sinners, and you wish to see them lost.   Fire, indeed ! and punishment ! —speak no more of chastisements, for such a spirit is not Mine."   But of Mary, whose spirit is the same as that of her Son, we can never doubt that she is all-inclined to mercy ; for, as she said to St. Bridget, she is called the Mother of mercy, and it was by God's own mercy that she was made thus compassionate and sweet towards all : " I am called the mother of mercy, and truly God's mercy made me thus merciful." † For this reason Mary was seen by St. John clothed with the sun : " And a great sign appeared in heaven, a woman clothed with the sun." ‡   On which words St. Bernard, turning towards the Blessed Virgin, says, " Thou, O Lady, hast clothed the sun, that is the Eternal Word, with human flesh ; but He has clothed thee with His power and mercy." §

" This Queen," continues the same St. Bernard, " is so compassionate and benign, that when a sinner, whoever he may be, recommends himself to her charity, she does not question his merits, or whether he is worthy or unworthy to be attended to, but she hears and succors all." ‖   " And therefore," remarks St. Idelbert, " Mary is said to be ' fair as the moon.' " ¶   For as the moon enlightens and benefits the lowest creatures on earth, so does Mary enlighten and succor the most unworthy sinners.   " And though the moon," says another writer, " receives all its light from the sun, yet

---

* Luke ix. 55.   † Rev. l. 2. c. 23.   ‡ Apoc. xii. 1.
§ *In Sign. Magn.*   ‖ *In Sign. Magn.*   ¶ Cant. vi. 9.

it works quicker than the sun; for what this latter does in a year the moon does in a month." * For this reason St. Anselm says "that we often more quickly obtain what we ask by calling on the name of Mary than by invoking that of Jesus." † On this subject Hugo of St. Victor remarks, that "though our sins may cause us to fear to approach the Almighty, because it is His infinite majesty that we have offended, we must never fear to go to Mary, for in her we shall find nothing to terrify us. True it is that she is holy, immaculate, and the Queen of the world; but she is also of our flesh, and, like us, a child of Adam." ‡

"In fine," says St. Bernard, "all that belongs to Mary is filled with grace and mercy, for she, as a Mother of mercy, has made herself all to all, and out of her most abundant charity she has made herself a debtor to the wise and the foolish, to the just and sinners, and opens to all her compassionate heart, that all may receive the fulness of its treasures." § So much so, that as "the devil," according to St. Peter, "goes about seeking whom he may devour," ‖ so, on the other hand, says Bernardine de Bustis, does Mary go about seeking whom she may save, and to whom she may give life.¶

We should fully understand and always bear in mind a remark of St. Germanus, who says, "that the protection of Mary is greater and more powerful than anything of which we can form an idea." ** "How is it," asks another writer, "that that Lord who under the old dispensation was so rigorous in his punishments,

---

* *Joann. a S. Gem. Summ.* l. I, c. 3.
† *De Excell. V.* c. 6.   ‡ *Spinelli, M. Deip.* c. 30, n. 12.
§ *In Sign. Magn.*   ‖ I Pet. v. 8.
¶ *Marial.* p. 3, s. I.   ** *De Zona Deip.*

now shows such mercy to persons guilty of far greater
crimes?" And he answers, "that it is all for the love
of Mary, and on account of her merits." * "Oh, how
long since," exclaims St. Fulgentius, " would the world
have been destroyed, had not Mary sustained it by her
powerful intercession!" † "But now," says Arnold
of Chartres, "that we have the Son as our mediator
with the Eternal Father, and the Mother as a mediatress with the Son, we have full access, and can go to
God with entire confidence and hope for every good
thing." "How," he goes on to say, "can the Father
refuse to hear the Son who shows Him His side and
wounds, the marks of His sufferings endured for sinners ; and how can the Son refuse to hear His Mother
when she shows Him her bosom and the breasts that
gave Him suck?" ‡ St. Peter Chrysologus says,
"that a gentle maiden having lodged a God in her
womb, asks as its price peace for the world, salvation
for those who are lost, and life for the dead." §

"Oh, how many," exclaims the Abbot of Celles, "who
deserve to be condemned by the justice of the Son,
are saved by the mercy of the Mother ! for she is God's
treasure, and the treasurer of all graces ; and thus our
salvation is in her hands, and depends on her." ‖ Let
us, then, always have recourse to this compassionate
Mother, and confidently hope for salvation through
her intercession ; for she, according to the encouraging
assurance of Bernardine de Bustis, " is our salvation,
our life, our hope, our counsel, our refuge, our help." ¶
"Mary," says St. Antoninus,** "is that throne of
grace to which the apostle St. Paul, in his epistle

---

* *Pelbart, Stell.* l. 11, p. 2, c. 2.   † *Pelbart, loco cit.*
‡ *De Laud. B. V.*   § Serm. 140. ‖ *Cont. de V. M. in prol.*
¶ *Marial.* p. 1, s. 6.   ** P. 4, t. 15, c. 14, § 7.

to the Hebrews, exhorts us to fly with confidence, that we may obtain the divine mercy, and all the help we need for our salvation." " Let us therefore go with confidence to the throne of grace : that we may obtain mercy, and find grace in seasonable aid." * " To the throne of grace, that is, to Mary," says St. Antoninus ; and for this reason St. Catherine of Siena called Mary " the dispenser of divine mercy." †

Let us conclude with the beautiful and tender exclamation of St. Bonaventure on these words, " O merciful, O compassionate, O sweet Virgin Mary ! " " O Mary, thou art clement with the miserable, compassionate towards those who pray to thee, sweet towards those who love thee ; clement with the penitent, compassionate to those who advance, sweet to the perfect. Thou showest thyself clement in delivering us from chastisement, compassionate in bestowing graces, and sweet in giving thyself to those who seek thee." ‡

Prayer.

O Mother of mercy, since thou art so compassionate, and hast so great a desire to render service to us poor creatures and to grant our requests, behold I, the most miserable of all men, have now recourse to thy compassion, in order that thou mayest grant me that which I ask. Others may ask what they please of thee,—bodily health, and earthly goods and advantages ; but I come, O Lady, to ask thee for that which thou desirest of me, and which is most in conformity and agreeable to thy most sacred heart. Thou art so humble ; obtain for me humility and love of contempt. Thou wast so patient under the sufferings of this life ; obtain for me patience in trials. Thou wast all filled with the love of God ; obtain for me the

* Heb. iv. 16. † *Or. in Annunt.* ‡ *Med. in Salve Reg.*

gift of His pure and holy love.   Thou wast all love towards thy neighbor; obtain for me charity towards all, and particularly towards those who are in any way my enemies. Thou wast entirely united to the divine will; obtain for me entire conformity to the will of God in whatever way He may be pleased to dispose of me.   Thou, in fine, art the most holy of all creatures; O Mary, make me a saint. Love for me is not wanting on thy part; thou canst do all, and thou hast the will to obtain me all.   The only thing, then, that can prevent me from receiving thy graces is, either neglect on my part in having recourse to thee, or little confidence in thy intercession; but these two things thou must obtain for me.   These two greatest graces I ask from thee; from thee I must obtain them; from thee I hope for them with the greatest confidence, O Mary, my Mother Mary, my hope, my love, my life, my refuge, my help, and my consolation.   Amen.

CHAPTER X.

O dulcis Virgo Maria.

O SWEET VIRGIN MARY.

SWEETNESS OF THE NAME OF MARY.

The Sweetness of the Name of Mary during Life and Death.

THE great name of Mary, which was given to the divine Mother, did not come to her from her parents, nor was it given to her by the mind or will of man, as is the case with all other names that are imposed in this world ; but it came from heaven, and was given her by a divine ordinance. This is attested by St. Jerome,* St. Epiphanius,† St. Antoninus,‡ and others. "The name of Mary came from the treasury of the divinity," § says St. Peter Damian. Ah, yes, O Mary, it was from that treasury that thy high and admirable name came forth ; for the Most Blessed Trinity, says Richard of St. Laurence, bestowed on thee a name above every other name after that of thy Son, and ennobled it with such majesty and power that all heaven, earth, and hell, on only hearing it, should fall down and venerate it. But I will give the author's own words : "The whole Trinity, O Mary, gave thee a name after that of thy Son above every

* *De Nat. M. V.*   † *Or. de Præs. Deip.*
‡ *Hist.* p. 1, t. 4. c. 6, § 10.   § *S. de Annunt.*

other name, that in thy name every knee should bow, of things in heaven, on earth, and under the earth." * But amongst the other privileges of the name of Mary, and which were given to it by God, we will now examine that of the peculiar sweetness found in it by the servants of this most holy Lady during life and in death.

And in the first place, speaking of the course of our life, the holy anchorite Honorius used to say, that " this name of Mary is filled with every sweetness and divine savor ; " † so much so that the glorious St. Anthony of Padua found the same sweetness in the name of Mary that St. Bernard found in that of Jesus. " Name of Jesus ! " exclaimed the one. " O name of Mary ! " replied the other ; " joy in the heart, honey in the mouth, melody to the ear of her devout clients." ‡ It is narrated in the life of the venerable Father Juvenal Ancina, Bishop of Saluzzo, that in pronouncing the name of Mary he tasted so great and sensible a sweetness that, after doing so, he licked his lips. We read also that a lady at Cologne told the Bishop Massilius that as often as she uttered the name of Mary she experienced a taste far sweeter than honey. The bishop imitated her, and experienced the same thing.§

We gather from the sacred canticles that on the Assumption of our blessed Lady the angels asked her name three times. " Who is she that goeth up by the desert as a pillar of smoke ? " ‖ Again : " Who is she that cometh forth as the morning rising ? " ¶ And

---

* *De Laud. B. M.* l. 1, c. 2.

† *Ap. Lyr. Tris. Mar.* l. 2, m. 13.

‡ *Dom.* 3 *Quadr.* s. 2.   § *Cæsarius, Dial.* l. 7, c. 50.

‖ Cant. iii. 6.   ¶ *Ib.* vi. 9.

again: " Who is this that cometh up from the desert, flowing with delights ? " *   " And why," says Richard of St. Laurence, " do the angels so often ask the name of their Queen ? "   He answers, " That it was so sweet even to the angels to hear it pronounced that they desired to hear that sweet name in reply." †

But here I do not intend to speak of that sensible sweetness, for it is not granted to all ; I speak of that salutary sweetness of consolation, of love, of joy, of confidence, of strength, which the name of Mary ordinarily brings to those who pronounce it with devotion.

The Abbot Francone, speaking on this subject, says: " There is no other name after that of the Son, in heaven or on earth, whence pious minds derive so much grace, hope, and sweetness."   After the most sacred name of Jesus, the name of Mary is so rich in every good thing that on earth and in heaven there is no other from which devout souls receive so much grace, hope, and sweetness.   " For," he continues, " there is something so admirable, sweet, and divine in this name of Mary that when it meets with friendly hearts it breathes into them an odor of delightful sweetness."   And he adds, in conclusion, " that the wonder of this great name is, that if heard by the lovers of Mary a thousand times, it is always heard again with renewed pleasure, for they always experience the same sweetness each time it is pronounced." ‡

The Blessed Henry Suso,§ also speaking of this sweetness, says, " that when he named Mary he felt himself so excited to confidence, and inflamed with

* Cant. viii. 5.   † *De Laud. V. M.* l. 1, c. 2.
‡ *De Grat. D.* l. 6.   § *Dial.* c. 16.

such love and joy, that between the tears and joy
with which he pronounced the beloved name he desired that his heart might leave his breast ; for he
declared that this most sweet name was like a honey-
comb dissolving in the inmost recess of the soul ; "
and then he would exclaim : " O most sweet name !
O Mary, what must thou thyself be, since thy name
alone is thus amiable and gracious ! "

The enamoured St. Bernard, raising his heart to his
good Mother, says with tenderness, " O great! O pious!
O thou who art worthy of all praise ! O most holy
Virgin Mary ! Thy name is so sweet and amiable that
it cannot be pronounced without inflaming those who
do so with love towards thee and God.   It only need
occur to the thought of thy lovers to move them to
love thee more, and to console them."   " Thou canst
not be named without inflaming; thou canst not be
thought of by those who love thee without filling
their minds with joy." *   " And if riches comfort
the poor, because they relieve them in their distress,
oh, how much more does thy name, O Mary," says
Richard of St. Laurence, " comfort us than any earthly
riches!   It comforts us in the anguishes of this life."
" Thy name, O Mary, is far better than riches, because
it can better relieve poverty." †

In fine, " thy name, O Mother of God, is filled with
divine graces and blessings," ‡ as St. Methodius says.
So much so that St. Bonaventure declares, " that thy
name, O Mary, cannot be pronounced without bringing some grace to him who does so devoutly."§   The
Blessed Raymond Jordano says that however hard-

* *Depr. gl. V.*   † *De Laud. B. M.* l. 1, c. 2,
‡ *De Sim. et Anna.*   § *Spec. B. V. lect.* 9.

ened and diffident a heart may be, the name of the most blessed Virgin has such efficacy that if it is only pronounced that heart will be wonderfully softened. I will, however, give his own words : " The power of thy most holy name, O ever-blessed Virgin Mary, is such that it softens the hardness of the human heart in a wonderful manner." He then tells us that it is she who leads sinners to the hope of pardon and grace: " By thee does the sinner recover the hope of forgiveness and of grace." *

Thy most sweet name, O Mary, according to St. Ambrose, " is a precious ointment, which breathes forth the odor of divine grace." The saint then prays to the divine Mother, saying : " Let this ointment of salvation enter the inmost recesses of our souls ; " † that is, Grant, O Lady, that we may often remember to name thee with love and confidence ; for this practice either shows the possession of divine grace, or else is a pledge that we shall soon recover it. " And truly it is so, O Mary ; for the remembrance of thy name comforts the afflicted, recalls those who have erred to the way of salvation, and encourages sinners, that they may not abandon themselves to despair." It is thus that Ludolph of Saxony addresses her.‡

Father Pelbart says, " that as Jesus Christ by His five wounds gave a remedy for the evils of the world, so also does Mary, by her most holy name, which is composed of five letters, daily bring pardon to sinners." §

For this reason is the holy name of Mary likened in the sacred Canticles to oil : " Thy name is as oil

---

* *Cont. de V. M.* c. 5.　　　† *Instit. Virg.* c. 13.
‡ *Vita Chr.* p. 2, c. 86.　　§ *Stell.* l. 6, p. 1, a. 2.

poured out." * On these words Blessed Alan says that the glory of her name is compared to oil poured out ; because oil heals the sick, sends out a sweet odor, and nourishes flames.† Thus also does the name of Mary heal sinners, rejoice hearts, and inflame them with divine love. Hence Richard of St. Laurence " encourages sinners to have recourse to this great name," because it alone will suffice to cure them of all their evils ; and " there is no disorder, however malignant, that does not immediately yield to the power of the name of Mary." ‡

On the other hand, Thomas à Kempis affirms " that the devils fear the Queen of heaven to such a degree that only on hearing her great name pronounced they fly from him who does so as from a burning fire." § The Blessed Virgin herself revealed to St. Bridget " that there is not on earth a sinner, however devoid he may be of the love of God, from whom the devil is not obliged immediately to fly, if he invokes her holy name with a determination to repent." On another occasion she repeated the same thing to the saint, saying, " that all the devils venerate and fear her name to such a degree that on hearing it they immediately loosen the claws with which they hold the soul captive." Our blessed Lady also told St. Bridget, " that in the same way as the rebel angels fly from sinners who invoke the name of Mary, so also do the good angels approach nearer to just souls who pronounce her name with devotion." ‖

St. Germanus declares, " that as breathing is a sign of life, so also is the frequent pronunciation of the name of Mary a sign either of the life of divine grace,

* *Off. B. V. resp.* 6. † *In Cant.* i.
‡ *De Laud. B. M.* l. 1, c. 2. § *Ad Nov.* s. 23. ‖ Rev. l. 1, c. 9.

or that it will soon come ; for this powerful name has in it the virtue of obtaining help and life for him who invokes it devoutly." Addressing the Blessed Virgin, he says : " As breathing is a sign of life in the body, so is the frequent repetition of thy most holy name, O Virgin, by thy servants not only a sign of life and of strength, but also it procures and conciliates both." *

In fine, " this admirable name of our sovereign Lady," says Richard of St. Laurence, " is like a fortified tower, in which, if a sinner takes refuge, he will be delivered from death ; for it defends and saves even the most abandoned." But it is a tower of strength, which not only delivers sinners from chastisement, but also defends the just from the assaults of hell. Thus the same Richard says, " that, after the name of Jesus, there is no other in which men find so powerful assistance and salvation as in the great name of Mary." †
He says, " There is not such powerful help in any name, nor is there any other name given to men, after that of Jesus, from which so much salvation is poured forth upon men as from the name of Mary." Moreover, it is well known, and is daily experienced by the clients of Mary, that her powerful name gives the particular strength necessary to overcome temptations against purity. The same author in his commentary on the words of St. Luke, " and the virgin's name was Mary,"‡ remarks that these two words, Mary and virgin, are joined together by the evangelist to denote that the name of this most pure Virgin should always be coupled with the virtue of chastity. § Hence St. Peter Chrysologus says, " that the name of Mary is an indication of chastity," ‖ meaning, that when we doubt as

---

* *De Zona Deip.*   † *De Laud. B. M.* l. 11.
‡ Luke i. 27.   § *Loco cit.*   ‖ *Serm.* 146.

to whether we have consented to thoughts against this virtue, if we remember having invoked the name of Mary, we have a certain proof that we have not sinned.

Let us, therefore, always take advantage of the beautiful advice given us by St. Bernard, in these words : " In dangers, in perplexities, in doubtful cases think of Mary, call on Mary ; let her not leave thy lips ; let her not depart from thy heart." * In every danger of forfeiting divine grace we should think of Mary, and invoke her name, together with that of Jesus ; for these two names always go together. Oh, then, never let us permit these two most sweet names to leave our hearts, or be off our lips ; for they will give us strength not only not to yield, but to conquer all our temptations.

Consoling indeed are the promises of help made by Jesus Christ to those who have devotion to the name of Mary ; for one day in the hearing of St. Bridget He promised His most holy Mother that He would grant three special graces to those who invoke that holy name with confidence : first, that He would grant them perfect sorrow for their sins ; secondly, that their crimes should be atoned for ; and, thirdly, that He would give them strength to attain perfection, and at length the glory of paradise. And then our divine Saviour added : " For thy words, O My Mother, are so sweet and agreeable to Me that I cannot deny what thou askest." †

St. Ephrem goes so far as to say "that the name of Mary is the key of the gates of heaven," ‡ in the hands

---

* *De Laud. V. M.* hom. 2.   † Rev. l. 1, c. 50.
‡ *De Laud. Dei Gen.*

of those who devoutly invoke it. And thus it is not without reason that St. Bonaventure says " that Mary is the salvation of all who call upon her : " for he addresses her, saying : " O salvation of all who invoke thee ! " meaning, that to obtain eternal salvation and invoke her name are synonymous ; and Richard of St. Laurence affirms, " that the devout invocation of this sweet and holy name leads to the acquisition of superabundant graces in this life, and a very high degree of glory in the next." * " If, then, O brethren," concludes Thomas à Kempis, " you desire consolation in every labor, have recourse to Mary, invoke the name of Mary, honor Mary, recommend yourselves to Mary, rejoice with Mary, weep with Mary, pray with Mary, walk with Mary, seek Jesus with Mary ; in fine, desire to live and die with Jesus and Mary. By acting thus you will always advance in the ways of God, for Mary will most willingly pray for you, and the Son will most certainly grant all that His Mother asks." †

Thus we see that the most holy name of Mary is sweet indeed to her clients during life, on account of the very great graces that she obtains for them. But sweeter still will it be to them in death, on account of the tranquil and holy end that it will insure them.

Father Sertorius Caputo, of the Society of Jesus, exhorted all who assist the dying frequently to pronounce the name of Mary ; for this name of life and hope, when repeated at the hour of death, suffices to put the devils to flight, and to comfort such persons in their sufferings.

St. Camillus of Lellis also recommended his relig-

* *De Laud. B. M.* l. 1, c. 2. † *Ad Nov.* s. 21.

ious, in the strongest terms, to remind the dying frequently to invoke the names of Jesus and Mary. This was his own custom when attending others ; but oh, how sweetly did he practise it himself on his death-bed, for then he pronounced the beloved names of Jesus and Mary with such tenderness that he even inflamed those who heard him with love, and at length, with his eyes fixed on their venerated images, and his arms in the form of a cross, the saint breathed forth his soul with an air of holiness and in the midst of heavenly peace, in the very moment that he was pronouncing those sweet names.

" The invocation of the sacred names of Jesus and Mary," says Thomas à Kempis, " is a short prayer which is as sweet to the mind, and as powerful to protect those who use it against the enemies of their salvation, as it is easy to remember." *

" Blessed is the man who loves thy name, O Mary," exclaims St. Bonaventure. " Yes, truly blessed is he who loves thy sweet name, O Mother of God ! for," he continues, " thy name is so glorious and admirable that no one who remembers it has any fears at the hour of death." †   Such is its power that none of those who invoke it at the hour of death fear the assaults of their enemies.

Oh, that we may end our lives as did the Capuchin Father, Fulgentius of Ascoli, who expired singing, " O Mary, O Mary, the most beautiful of creatures ! let us depart together ; " or, according to the annals of the Order, like Blessed Henry the Cistercian, who expired in the very moment that he was pronouncing the most sweet name of Mary.

* *Vall. lil.* c. 13.   † *Psalt. B. V. ps.* i. 110.

Let us then, O devout reader, beg God to grant us that at death the name of Mary may be the last word on our lips. This was the prayer of St. Germanus : " May the last movement of my tongue be to pronounce the name of the Mother of God ! " * Oh, sweet, oh, safe is that death which is accompanied and protected by so saving a name ; for God grants the grace of invoking it only to those whom He is about to save.

O my sweet Lady and Mother, I love thee much, and because I love thee I also love thy holy name. I purpose and hope, with thy assistance, always to invoke it during life and at death. And to conclude with the tender prayer of St. Bonaventure : "I ask thee, O Mary, for the glory of thy name, to come and meet my soul when it is departing from this world, and to take it in thine arms. Disdain not, O Mary, to come then and comfort me with thy presence. Be thyself my soul's ladder and way to heaven. Do thou thyself obtain for it the grace of forgiveness and eternal repose. O Mary, our advocate, it is for thee to defend thy clients, and to undertake their cause before the tribunal of Jesus Christ." †

Prayer.

O great Mother of God and my Mother Mary, it is true that I am unworthy to name thee ; but thou, who lovest me and desirest my salvation, must, notwithstanding the impurity of my tongue, grant that I may always invoke thy most holy and powerful name in my aid, for thy name is the succor of the living, and the salvation of the dying. Ah, most pure Mary, most sweet Mary, grant that hence-

* *In Deip. Ann.* † *Psalt. B. V. ps.* 113.

forth thy name may be the breath of my life. O Lady, delay not to help me when I invoke thee, for in all the temptations which assail me, and in all my wants, I will never cease calling upon thee, and repeating again and again, Mary, Mary. Thus it is that I hope to act during my life, and more particularly at death, that after that last struggle I may eternally praise thy beloved name in heaven, O clement, O pious, O sweet Virgin Mary. Ah, Mary, most amiable Mary, with what consolation, what sweetness, what confidence, what tenderness, is my soul penetrated in only naming, in only thinking of thee! I thank my Lord and God, who, for my good, has given thee a name so sweet and deserving of love, and at the same time so powerful. But, my sovereign Lady, I am not satisfied with only naming thee, I wish to name thee with love : I desire that my love may every hour remind me to call on thee, so that I may be able to exclaim with St. Bonaventure," O name of the Mother of God, thou art my love." * " My own dear Mary, O my beloved Jesus, may your most sweet names reign in my heart, and in all hearts. Grant that I may forget all others to remember, and always invoke, your adorable names alone. Ah ! Jesus my Redeemer, and my Mother Mary, when the moment of death comes when I must breathe forth my soul and leave this world, deign, through your merits, to grant that I may then pronounce my last words, and that they may be, " I love Thee, O Jesus ; I love thee, O Mary ; to you do I give my heart and my soul."

* *Med. de Sal. B. V.*

APPENDIX.

PRACTICES OF DEVOTION
IN HONOR OF THE DIVINE MOTHER.

From Part Five of The Glories of Mary. *(Imprimatur* ✠ *Patrick
Cardinal Hayes, Archbishop of New York,* April 16, 1931.)

"THE Queen of Heaven is so gracious and liberal,"
says St. Andrew of Crete, "that she recompenses her
servants with the greatest munificence for the most tri-
fling devotions."[1] Two conditions, however, there are:

The first is that when we offer her our devotions our
souls should be free from sin; otherwise she would
address us as she addressed a wicked soldier spoken
of by St. Peter Celestine.[2] This soldier every day performed some devotion in honor of our Blessed Lady.
One day he was suffering greatly from hunger, when
Mary appeared to him and offered him some most deli-
cious meats, but in so filthy a vessel that he could not
bring himself to taste them. "I am the mother of God,"
the Blessed Virgin then said, "and am come to satisfy
thy hunger." "But, O Lady," he answered, "I cannot
eat out of so dirty a vessel." "And how," replied Mary,
"canst thou expect that I should accept thy devotions
offered to me with so defiled a soul as thine?" On hearing this the soldier was converted, became a hermit,
and lived in a desert for thirty years. At death the
Blessed Virgin again appeared to him and took him her-

1. *In Dorm. B. V.* s. 3.   2. *Opusc.* 6, c. 23.

self to heaven. In the first part of this work[3] we said that it was morally impossible for a client of Mary to be lost; but this must be understood on condition that he lives either without sin, or, at least, with the desire to abandon it; for then the Blessed Virgin will help him. But should any one, on the other hand, sin in the hope that Mary will save him, he thereby would render himself unworthy and incapable of her protection.

The second condition is perseverance in devotion to Mary: "Perseverance alone," says St. Bernard, "will merit a crown."[4] When Thomas à Kempis was a young man he used every day to have recourse to the Blessed Virgin with certain prayers; he one day omitted them; he then omitted them for some weeks, and finally gave them up altogether. One night he saw Mary in a dream: she embraced all his companions, but when his turn came, she said, "What dost thou expect, thou who hast given up thy devotions? Depart, thou art unworthy of my caresses." On hearing this Thomas awoke in alarm, and resumed his ordinary prayers.[5] Hence, Richard of St. Laurence with reason says that "he who perseveres in his devotion to Mary will be blessed in his confidence and will obtain all he desires."[6] But as no one can be certain of this perseverance, no one before death can be certain of salvation. The advice given by the Venerable [now *Saint*] John Berchmans, of the Society of Jesus, deserves our particular attention. When this holy young man was dying his companions entreated him, before he left this world, to tell them what devotion they could perform which would be most agreeable to our Blessed Lady. He replied in the following remarka-

3. Chapter VIII.
4. *Epist.* 129.
5. *Auriemma, Aff. Scamb.* p. I, c. 4.
6. *De Laud. B. M.* 1. 2, p. I.

ble words: "Any devotion, however small, provided it is constant." I therefore now give with simplicity, and in a few words, the various devotions which we can offer to our Mother in order to obtain her favor; and this I consider the most useful part of my work. But I do not so much recommend my dear reader to practice them all as to choose those which please him most, and to persevere in them, for fear that if he omits them he may lose the protection of the divine Mother. Oh, how many are there now in hell who would have been saved had they only persevered in the devotions which they once practiced in honor of Mary!

The Hail Mary.

This angelical salutation is most pleasing to the ever-blessed Virgin; for, whenever she hears it, it would seem as if the joy which she experienced when St. Gabriel announced to her that she was the chosen Mother of God was renewed to her; and with this object in view, we should often salute her with the "Hail Mary." "Salute her," says Thomas à Kempis, "with the angelical salutation, for she indeed hears this sound with pleasure."[7] The divine Mother herself told St. Matilda that no one could salute her in a manner more agreeable to herself than with the "Hail Mary."[8]

He who salutes Mary will also be saluted by her. St. Bernard once heard a statue of the Blessed Virgin salute him, saying, "Hail, Bernard." Mary's salutation, says St. Bonaventure, will always be some grace corresponding to the wants of him who salutes her: "She willingly salutes us with grace, if we willingly salute her with a Hail Mary."[9] Richard of Laurence adds,

7. *Ad Novit.* s. 2I.
8. *Spir. Grat.* l. I, c. 67.
9. *Spec. B. V. lect.* 4.

"that if we address the Mother of our Lord, saying, 'Hail Mary,' she cannot refuse the grace which we ask."[10] Mary herself promised St. Gertrude as many graces at death as she would have said "Hail Marys."[11] Blessed Alan asserts, "that as all heaven rejoices when the 'Hail Mary' is said, so also do the devils tremble and take flight."[12] This Thomas à Kempis affirms on his own experience; for he says that once the devil appeared to him, and instantly fled on hearing the "Hail Mary."[13]

To practice this devotion:

1. We can every morning and evening on rising and going to bed say three "Hail Marys" prostrate, or at least kneeling; and add to each "Hail Mary" this short prayer: *O Mary, by thy pure and immaculate conception, make my body pure and my soul holy.*[14] We should then, as St. Stanislaus always did, ask Mary's blessing as our Mother; place ourselves under the mantle of her protection, beseeching her to guard us during the coming day or night from sin. For this purpose it is advisable to have a beautiful picture or image of the Blessed Virgin.

2. We can say the *Angelus* with the usual three "Hail Marys" in the morning, at mid-day, and in the evening. Pope John XXII. was the first to grant an indulgence for this devotion; it was on the following occasion, as Father Crasset relates:[15] A criminal was condemned to be burned alive on the vigil of the Annunciation of the Mother of God: he saluted her with a "Hail Mary," and

10. *De Laud. B. M.* l. I, c. 8.
11. *Insin.* l. 4, c. 53.
12. *De Psalt.* l. 4, c. 30.
13. *Ad Novit.* s. 21.
14. 300 days Indulgence, morning and evening.
15. *Vér. Dév.* p. 2, tr. 6, p. 2.

in the midst of the flames he, and even his clothes, remained uninjured. In 1724, Benedict XIII. granted a hundred days' indulgence to all who recite it, and a plenary indulgence once a month to those who during that time have recited it daily as above, on condition of going to confession and receiving Holy Communion, and praying for the usual intentions. At the end of each "Hail Mary" may be added "Thanks be to God and to Mary." Formerly, at the sound of the bell, all knelt down to say the "Angelus"; but in the present day there are some who are ashamed to do so. St. Charles Borromeo was not ashamed to leave his carriage or get off his horse to say the "Angelus" in the street, and even sometimes in the mud. It is related that there was a slothful religious who neglected to kneel at the sound of the Angelus bell; he saw the belfry bow down three times, and a voice said, "Behold, wilt thou not do that which even inanimate creatures do?"[16] Here we must remark that Benedict XIV. directed that in paschal time, instead of saying the "Angelus," we should say the "Regina Caeli"; and that on Saturday evenings, and the whole of Sunday, the "Angelus" should be said standing.

We can salute the Mother of God with a "Hail Mary" every time we hear the clock strike. Blessed Alphonsus Rodriguez saluted her every hour; and at night, angels awoke him, that he might not omit this devotion.

4. In going out and returning to the house we can salute the Blessed Virgin with a "Hail Mary," that both at home and abroad she may guard us from all sin; and we should each time kiss her feet, as the Carthusian Fathers always do.

5. We should reverence every image of Mary which

16. *Auriemma, Aff.* p. 1, c. 3.

we pass with a "Hail Mary." For this purpose those who
can do so would do well to place a beautiful image of
the Blessed Virgin on the wall of their houses, that it
may be venerated by those who pass. In Naples, and
still more in Rome, there are most beautiful images of
our Blessed Lady placed by the wayside by her devout
clients.

6. By command of the holy Church all the canonical
hours are preceded by a "Hail Mary," and concluded
with it; we therefore do well to begin and end all our
actions with a "Hail Mary." I say all our actions,
whether spiritual, such as prayer, confession, and Communion, spiritual reading, hearing sermons, and the
like; or temporal, such as study, giving advice, working,
going to table, to bed, etc. Happy are those actions that
are enclosed between two "Hail Marys." So also should
we do on waking in the morning, on closing our eyes to
sleep, in every temptation, in every danger, in every
inclination to anger, and the like; on these occasions we
should always say a "Hail Mary."

My dear reader, do this, and you will see the immense
advantage that you will derive from it. Father
Auriemma relates that the Blessed Virgin promised St.
Matilda a happy death if she every day recited three
"Hail Marys" in honor of her power, wisdom and goodness. Moreover, she herself told St. Jane Frances de
Chantal that the "Hail Mary" was most acceptable to
her, and especially when recited ten times in honor of
her ten virtues.

Novenas.

Devout clients of Mary are all attention and fervor in
celebrating the novenas, or nine days preceding her festivals; and the Blessed Virgin is all love in dispensing

innumerable and most special graces to them. St. Gertrude one day saw, under Mary's mantle, a band of souls whom the great Lady was considering with the most tender affection; and she was given to understand that they were persons who, during the preceding days, had prepared themselves with various devotions for the Feast of the Assumption.[17] The following devotions are some of those which may be used during the novenas:

1. We may make mental prayer in the morning and evening, and a visit to the Blessed Sacrament, adding nine times the "Our Father, Hail Mary, and Glory be to the Father."

2. We may pay Mary three visits (visiting her statue or picture), and thank our Lord for the graces that He granted her: and each time ask the Blessed Virgin for some special grace; in one of these visits the prayer which will be found after the discourse on the feast, whichever it may be, can be said.[18]

3. We may make many acts of love towards Mary (at least fifty or a hundred), and also towards Jesus; for we can do nothing that pleases her more than to love her Son, as she said to St. Bridget: "If thou wishest to bind thyself to me, love my Son."

4. We may read every day of the novena, for a quarter of an hour, some book that treats of her glories.

5. We may perform some external mortification, such as wearing a hair-cloth, taking a discipline, or the like; we can also fast, or at table abstain from fruit, or some favorite dish, at least a part of it, or chew some bitter herbs. On the vigil of the feast we may fast on bread and water: but none of these things should be done without the permission of our confessor. Interior mortifications, however, are the best of all to practice dur-

17. *Insin.* 1. 4, c. 50.   18. Part II of *The Glories of Mary.*

ing these novenas, such as to avoid looking at or listening to things out of curiosity; to remain in retirement; observe silence; be obedient; not give impatient answers; bear contradictions, and such things; which can all be practiced with less danger of vanity, with greater merit, and which do not need the confessor's permission. The most useful exercise is to propose, from the beginning of the novena, to correct some fault into which we fall the most frequently. For this purpose it will be well, in the visits spoken of above, to ask pardon for past faults, to renew our resolutions not to commit them any more, and to implore Mary's help. The devotion most dear and pleasing to Mary is to endeavor to imitate her virtues; therefore, it would be well always to propose to ourselves the imitation of some virtue that corresponds to the festival; as, for example, on the feast of her Immaculate Conception, purity of intention; on her Nativity, renewal of the spirit, to throw off tepidity; on her Presentation, detachment from something to which we are most attached; on her Annunciation, humility in supporting contempt; on her Visitation, charity towards our neighbor, in giving alms, or at least in praying for sinners; on her Purification, obedience to Superiors; and in fine, on the Feast of her Assumption, let us endeavor to detach ourselves from the world, do all to prepare ourselves for death, and regulate each day of our lives as if it was to be our last.

6. Besides going to Communion on the day of the feast, it would be well to ask leave from our confessor to go more frequently during the novena. Father Segneri used to say that we cannot honor Mary better than with Jesus. She herself revealed to a holy soul (as Father Crasset relates)[19] that we can offer her nothing

19. *Vér. Dév.* p. 2, tr. 6, pr. 6.

that is more pleasing to her than Holy Communion; for in that Holy Sacrament it is that Jesus gathers the fruit of His Passion in our soul. Hence it appears that the Blessed Virgin desires nothing so much of her clients as Communion, saying, *Come, eat my bread, and drink the wine which I have mingled for you.* (*Prov.* 9:5).

7. Finally, on the day of the feast, after Communion, we must offer ourselves to the service of this divine Mother, and ask of her the grace to practice the virtue, or whatever other grace we had proposed to ourselves, during the novena. It is well every year to choose, amongst the feasts of the Blessed Virgin, one for which we have the greatest and most tender devotion; and for this one to make a very special preparation by dedicating ourselves anew, and in a more particular manner, to her service, choosing her for our Sovereign Lady, Advocate, and Mother. Then we must ask her pardon for all our negligence in her service during the past year, and promise greater fidelity for the next; and conclude by begging her to accept us for her servants, and to obtain for us a holy death.

The Rosary and the Office of Our Blessed Lady.

It is well known that the devotion of the most holy Rosary was revealed to St. Dominic by the divine Mother herself, at a time when the saint was in affliction, and bewailing, with his Sovereign Lady, over the Albigensian heretics, who were at that time doing great mischief to the Church. The Blessed Virgin said to him: "This land will always be sterile until rain falls on it." St. Dominic was then given to understand that this rain was the devotion of the Rosary, which he was to propagate. This the saint indeed did, and it was embraced by all Catholics; so much so that, even to the present day, there is no devotion so generally practiced by the faithful of all classes as that of the Rosary. What is there that modern heretics, Calvin, Bucer, and others, have not said to throw discredit on the use of beads? But the immense good that this noble devotion has done to the world is well known. How many, by its means, have been delivered from sin! How many led to a holy life! How many to a good death, and are now saved! To be convinced of this, we need only read the many books that treat on the subject. Suffice it to know that this devotion has been approved by the Church, and that the Sovereign Pontiffs have enriched it with indulgences. . .The Rosary should also be said with devotion; and here we may call to mind what the Blessed Virgin said to St. Eulalia, "that she was better pleased with five decades said slowly and devoutly than with fifteen said in a hurry and with little devotion."[20] It is, therefore, well to say the Rosary kneeling, before an image of Mary, and, before each decade, to make an act of love to Jesus and Mary, and ask them for some particular grace. It is also preferable to say it with others rather than alone.

As to the Little Office of the Blessed Virgin, which is said to have been composed by St. Peter Damian, Pius V. granted indulgences to those who recited it, and the Blessed Virgin has many times shown how acceptable this devotion is to her, as may be seen in Father Auriemma's little work.[21]

She is also much pleased with the Litany of Loreto [Litany of the Blessed Virgin Mary], for reciting which there is an indulgence of three hundred days each time; and for those who say it every day, a plenary indulgence on Mary's five principal festivals—the Immaculate Con-

20. *Men. Cist.* 11 *Maii.*   21. *Aff. p.* 1, c. 8.

ception, Nativity, Annunciation, Purification, and Assumption, on the usual conditions. The hymn, *Ave Maris Stella*, "Hail Star of the Sea," is also very pleasing to Mary; she desired St. Bridget to say it every day;[22] but still more is she pleased with the *Magnificat*, for we then praise her in the very words in which she herself praised God.

Fasting.

There are many devout clients of Mary who, to honor her, fast on bread and water on Saturdays, and the vigils of her feasts.

It is well known that Saturday is dedicated by the holy Church to Mary, because, as St. Bernard says, on that day, the day after the death of her Son, she remained constant in faith.[23] Therefore, Mary's clients are careful to honor her on that day by some particular devotion, and especially by fasting on bread and water, as did St. Charles Borromeo, Cardinal Tolet, and so many others. Neithard, Bishop of Bamberg, and Father Joseph Arriaga, of the Society of Jesus, took no food at all on that day.

The great graces that the Mother of God has dispensed to those who do this are recorded by Father Auriemma in his little work.[24] Let one example suffice: it is that of a famous captain of brigands, who, on account of this devotion, was preserved in life after his head had been cut off, and was thus enabled to make his confession; for the unfortunate creature was in a state of sin. After confession he declared that, on account of this devotion, the Blessed Virgin had

22. *Rev. extr.* c. 8. 24. *Aff.* p. I, c. 17.
23. *Lib. de Pass.* c. 2.

obtained for him so great a grace, and immediately expired.

It would not, then, be anything very great for a person who pretends to be devout to Mary, and particularly for one who has perhaps already deserved hell, to offer her this fast on Saturdays. I affirm that those who practice this devotion can hardly be lost; not that I mean to say that if they die in mortal sin the Blessed Virgin will deliver them by a miracle, as she did this bandit: these are prodigies of divine mercy which very rarely occur, and it would be the height of folly to expect eternal salvation by such means; but I say that for those who practice this devotion, the divine Mother will make perseverance in God's grace easy, and obtain for them a good death. All the members of our little Congregation who are able to do so practice this devotion. I say those who are able to do so; for if our health does not permit it, at least we should on Saturdays content ourselves with one dish, or observe an ordinary fast, or abstain from fruit or something for which we have a relish. On Saturdays we should always practice some devotion in honor of our Blessed Lady, receive Holy Communion, or at least hear Mass, visit an image of Mary, wear a hair-cloth, or something of that sort. But at least on the vigils of her seven principal festivals her clients should offer her this fast either on bread and water, or honor her otherwise as best they can.

The Scapular.

As men esteem it an honor to have persons who wear their livery, so also is our Blessed Lady pleased that her clients should wear her scapular, as a mark that they have dedicated themselves to her service and that they are members of the household of the Mother of

God. Modern heretics, as usual, ridicule this devotion; but the holy Church has approved it by many Bulls and indulgences. Fathers Crasset and Lazzana,[25] speaking of the scapular of Mount Carmel, relate that towards the year 1251 the Blessed Virgin appeared to St. Simon Stock, an Englishman, and giving him the scapular, said that all who should wear it would be saved from eternal damnation. She said, "Receive, my beloved son, this scapular of thy Order, the badge of my confraternity, a privilege granted to thee and to all Carmelites: whoever dies clothed with it will not suffer eternal flames." Moreover, Father Crasset relates that Mary appeared to Pope John XXII., and commanded him to make it known that all those who should wear this scapular would be delivered from purgatory on the Saturday after their death; and this he did by a Bull, which was afterwards confirmed by Alexander V., Clement VII., and other Pontiffs. Paul V., as we have remarked in the first part of this work,[26] gives us to understand the same thing, and seems to explain the Bulls of his predecessors, and prescribes in his the conditions on which the indulgences may be gained. These conditions are: that each one should observe the chastity required in his state of life, and the recitation of the Little Office of the Blessed Virgin; those who cannot do so must be exact in keeping the fast days prescribed by the Church, and abstain from meat on Wednesdays and Saturdays.*

The indulgences, moreover, which are annexed to the

25. *Mar. Patr.* c. 5.   26. Page 183.

* These are the three conditions for obtaining the Sabbatine (Saturday) Privilege. The obligation of reciting the *Little Office of the Blessed Virgin Mary* can be commuted (changed) to another pious work—for example, the daily recitation of the Rosary, by any priest having diocesan faculties. By being

scapular of Mount Carmel, of the Seven Dolors of our Lady, of the Blessed Trinity, and especially of the Immaculate Conception, are innumerable, as well partial as plenary, both in life and for the hour of death. For my own part, I have been careful to receive all these scapulars. To that of the Immaculate Conception, in particular, very great indulgences have been attached by various sovereign pontiffs.

Frequent Recourse to Mary.

Of all devotions, there is none so pleasing to our Mother as that of having frequent recourse to her intercession, seeking her help in all our wants; for example, when we have to give or ask advice, in dangers, afflictions and temptations; and particularly in temptations against purity. The divine Mother will then certainly deliver us, if we have recourse to her by saying the antiphon, "We fly to thy patronage, etc."; or the "Hail Mary"; or by only invoking the most holy name of Mary, which has particular power against the devils.

Blessed Santi, of the Order of St. Francis, being once tempted with an impure thought, had recourse to Mary: she immediately appeared to him, and placing her hand on his breast delivered him.

It is also useful on these occasions to kiss or press to our heart our rosary or scapular, or to look at an image of the Blessed Virgin.

—End of excerpts from The Glories of Mary.—

enrolled in the Scapular of Mount Carmel (the "brown scapular"), a person becomes a member of the Scapular Confraternity, which is affiliated with the Carmelite Order. The enrollment is a brief ceremony which is performed by a priest.—*Publisher*, 1995.

Other Practices.

In *The Glories of Mary*, St. Alphonsus Liguori also sets forth a number of other pious practices in honor of Mary. These include visiting the images of Mary (including in one's own home); joining Confraternities dedicated to Our Lady; giving alms in Mary's honor, especially on Saturdays; saying Mass or hearing Mass or having Mass said in honor of the Blessed Virgin; saying the *Our Father, Hail Mary* and *Glory Be to the Father* three times each in honor of the Most Holy Trinity and in thanksgiving for the graces granted to Mary—for the Blessed Virgin, being unable to thank Our Lord for all the precious gifts He has bestowed on her, rejoices greatly when her children help her to thank God; reverencing the saints who are more nearly related to Mary, as St. Joseph, St. Joachim and St. Anne, and other saints who were especially devoted to Our Lady; reading each day a book that treats of the glories of Mary; trying to instill into all, particularly our relatives, devotion to Mary.

St. Alphonsus reminds his readers of the many indulgences available to those who in various ways honor the Queen of Heaven. He notes: "Those who endeavor to gain these indulgences must be careful to dispose themselves by an act of contrition."

PRAYERS TO THE
BLESSED VIRGIN MARY

Hail Holy Queen

(See the dedication page in the front of this book.)

Hail Mary

HAIL MARY, full of grace, the Lord is with thee; blessed art thou among women, and blessed is the fruit of thy womb, Jesus. Holy Mary, Mother of God, pray for us sinners, now and at the hour of our death. Amen.

We Fly to Thy Patronage

(Sub tuum praesidium)

WE FLY to thy patronage, O holy Mother of God; despise not our petitions in our necessities, but deliver us always from all dangers, O glorious and blessed Virgin.

The Angelus

The Angelus is traditionally recited morning (6:00 a.m.), noon and evening (6:00 p.m.) throughout the year except during Paschal time, when the Regina Caeli is recited instead.

V. The Angel of the Lord declared unto Mary.

R. And she conceived of the Holy Ghost. *Hail Mary,* etc.

V. Behold the handmaid of the Lord.

R. Be it done unto me according to thy word. *Hail Mary*, etc.

V. And the Word was made Flesh.

R. And dwelt among us. *Hail Mary*, etc.

V. Pray for us, O holy Mother of God,

R. That we may be made worthy of the promises of Christ.

Let Us Pray

Pour forth, we beseech Thee, O Lord, Thy grace into our hearts, that we to whom the Incarnation of Christ Thy Son was made known by the message of an angel, may by His Passion and Cross be brought to the glory of His Resurrection. Through the same Christ Our Lord. Amen.

The Regina Caeli

This prayer is recited morning, noon and evening during Paschal Time (from Easter through the evening of the Saturday after Pentecost) instead of The Angelus. It is traditionally recited standing.

V. Queen of Heaven, rejoice. Alleluia.

R. For He whom thou wast worthy to bear. Alleluia.

V. Has risen as He said. Alleluia.

R. Pray for us to God. Alleluia.

V. Rejoice and be glad, O Virgin Mary. Alleluia.

R. For the Lord is truly risen. Alleluia.

Let Us Pray

O God, Who by the Resurrection of Thy Son, Our Lord Jesus Christ, hast been pleased to give joy to the whole world, grant, we beseech Thee, that through the intercession of the Virgin Mary, His Mother, we may attain the joys of eternal life. Through the same Christ Our Lord. Amen.

The Magnificat
(Words of Our Lady from Luke 1:46-55.)

MY SOUL doth magnify the Lord, and my spirit hath rejoiced in God my Saviour, because He hath regarded the humility of His handmaid: for behold, from henceforth all generations shall call me blessed, because He that is mighty hath done great things to me, and holy is His Name. And His mercy is from generation unto generations, to them that fear Him.

He hath showed might in His arm: He hath scattered the proud in the conceit of their heart. He hath put down the mighty from their seat, and hath exalted the humble. He hath filled the hungry with good things, and the rich He hath sent empty away. He hath received Israel His servant, being mindful of His mercy: as He spoke to our fathers, to Abraham and to his seed forever.

The Memorare
(Famous Prayer of St. Bernard of Clairvaux)

REMEMBER, O most gracious Virgin Mary, that never was it known that anyone who fled to thy protection, implored thy help or sought thy intercession was left unaided. Inspired with this confidence, I fly unto thee, O Virgin of virgins, my Mother. To thee do I come, before thee I kneel, sinful and sorrowful. O Mother of the Word Incarnate, despise not my petitions, but in thy clemency hear and answer them. Amen.

Ave Maris Stella

HAIL thou star of ocean,
God's own Mother blest,
Ever sinless Virgin,
Gate of heavenly rest.

Oh! by Gabriel's Ave,
Uttered long ago,
Eva's name reversing
'Stablish peace below.

Break the captive's fetters,
Light on blindness pour;
All our ills expelling,
Every bliss implore.

Show thyself a Mother;
May the Word divine,
Born for us thine Infant,
Hear our prayers through thine.

Virgin all excelling,
Mildest of the mild;
Freed from guilt preserve us
Meek and undefiled.

Keep our life all spotless,
Make our way secure,
Till we find in Jesus,
Joy forevermore.

Through the highest Heaven
To the almighty Three,
Father, Son and Spirit
One same glory be. Amen.

Aspirations to Mary

O MARY, conceived without sin, pray for us who have recourse to thee.

HOLY MARY, pray for us!

IMMACULATE HEART of Mary, pray for us now and at the hour of our death.

SWEET HEART of Mary, be my salvation!

OUR LADY, Queen of Peace, pray for us!

Salve Regina

(Simple Tone)

Ant. 5.

Sál-ve Re-gí-na, * Ma-ter mi-se-ri-cór-di-æ, vi-ta, dul-cé-do et spes no-stra, sal-ve. Ad te cla-má-mus, éx-su-les, fí-li-i He-væ. Ad te su-spi-rá-mus, ge-mén-tes et flen-tes in hac la-cri-má-rum val-le. E-ia er-go, ad-vo-cá-ta no-stra, il-los tu-os mi-se-ri-cór-des ó-cu-los ad nos con-vér-te. Et Je-sum, be-ne-di-ctum fru-ctum ven-tris tu-i, no-bis post hoc ex-sí-li-um o-stén-de. O cle-mens, O pi-a, O dul-cis Vir-go Ma-rí-a.

If you have enjoyed this book, consider making your next selection from among the following . . .